Praise F

INTRODUCING YOUR CHILD TO SPORTS

"Who better to write this book than Dr. Ross Flowers? His experiences as a star youth athlete, college All-American and team captain at UCLA, and professional athlete—combined with his advanced education, sport psychology career, and being a father of three young athletes—may make him the best person to thoughtfully instruct parents on best practices and avoidable hazards in sport. It gives me great pride to know he's written a book that's needed for the youth community."

—Bob Larsen
2004 Olympic Coach USA Track & Field
UCLA Head Coach Track & Field

"Dr. Ross Flowers has a unique, positive, and laid-back style for introducing sports to kids. His approach was instrumental in my success as an Olympic gold medalist, and now, as a parent myself, Ross is helping me to introduce my children to sports and find creative ways to motivate them to be their best and to find a true athletic passion of their own."

—Chad Hedrick
2006, 2010 U.S. Olympic Speed Skater
2004, 2005 World Champion & 6x World Record Holder

"*Introducing Your Child to Sports* is an excellent step-by-step guide for parents to get children involved in playing sports, discover the benefits of doing so, and find the proper motivations for both parents and children. This book answers every question a parent could face at each phase of their child's involvement in athletics, and is definitely an extremely handy parental map for navigating the way to a child's positive and rewarding athletic experience."

—Apolo Anton Ohno
8x Olympic Medalist

INTRODUCING YOUR CHILD TO SPORTS

ISBN: 978-0-9961082-1-8

Published by:
GCG Publishing
Chula Vista, CA

Editing and book design by Stacey Aaronson

First Edition
Printed in the USA

INTRODUCING YOUR CHILD TO SPORTS

An Expert's Answers to Parents' Questions about Raising a Healthy, Balanced, Happy Athlete

ROSS FLOWERS, PHD

CONTENTS

Olympische Spiele München 1972

———

*T*his book is dedicated to my grandparents
Ross Ella Rydolph Giles, Leslie Eugene Giles, and Myrtle Bossett,
great-grandmother Myrtle Pitts,
and to my parents
Robert Flowers, Micki Flowers, and Vicki Giles Fabré—
everyday people with extraordinary talents,
who touched the lives of many.

I am extremely grateful for the sacrifices and commitments my elders made
to give me the opportunities to rise.
My fears are reduced and my confidence increased by embodying the lessons
they taught through selfless lives lived with purpose, courage, and love.

———

FOREWORD

It is extremely rare to find a professional like Dr. Ross Flowers who has the unique experience of being an elite-level competitive athlete, successful coach, and well-regarded sport psychologist. His ability to integrate his experience, instinct, knowledge, and educational background into a clear message that makes sense to athletes, coaches, and parents is spectacular. Though it's difficult to gain the trust of athletes and the respect of coaches, Dr. Flowers has continuously demonstrated his ability to gain both and, as a result, he makes a positive impact on performance. For many years, he has been an invaluable resource for me, as well as for the Olympic and Paralympic athletes I train.

I am thrilled that Dr. Flowers has written this book to share his expertise with the world, and I'm confident that parents and family members will find the information valuable. Through all of my years in sport as an Olympic champion, coach, and parent, my greatest athletic challenges have been within my own family—from trying to outperform my sister Jackie Joyner-Kersee, to keeping up with my late wife Florence Griffith-Joyner, to positively guiding the athleticism of my three children. It can be scary, heartbreaking, challenging, and frustrating, while at the same time exciting, fun,

encouraging, inspirational, and fulfilling. Because of my life experiences in sport, I want to provide my children with the best
opportunities to enjoy it—as I'm sure you do as well—and with
what I've learned from Dr. Flowers, I know I'm headed in the right
direction.

As you read this book, I hope you reap the same benefits I have
—benefits that will support your children on their journey
through the wide world of sports.

Enjoy!

—Al Joyner

Olympic Gold Medalist
First Family of Track & Field
1st American in 80 Years to Win Olympic Gold in the Triple Jump
1st African-American to Win Olympic Gold in the Triple Jump
USA High Performance Olympic Coach
Paralympic & USA Track & Field National Coach

PREFACE

As a child, I often went to sleep and awoke with visions of being in the Olympics, competing against the world's best athletes and being victorious. Since I was an average-sized kid, I didn't think there was anything particularly special about me that would allow me to be the next Olympic great, but I also didn't have any reason to doubt I could achieve what I dreamed. Like many kids, I didn't dream small—I envisioned being a great all-around athlete who excelled in multiple sports. I saw myself running as fast as Carl Lewis, playing basketball like Julius "Dr. J" Erving, and running through football defenders like Walter Payton. I had a great imagination.

My parents had a Jacob Lawrence poster depicting athletes running to the finish line in a relay competition at the 1972 Olympics in Munich, Germany. The image was specific to relay competition, yet when I looked at it, I mentally embellished the illustration by seeing myself successfully competing in various track and field sprinting events, soccer games, and basketball games against the world's greatest competitors. I knew at an early age that I would be a successful athlete. I could feel it.

As the parent of a young child yourself, you may have your own budding sports star. Conversely, you may have a reluctant child, one who has interest but feels held back by lack of talent, or one who has talent but no interest. You may likewise have a child who very much wants to play a sport, but your own concerns and questions are causing hesitation. For all of these scenarios and those that fall somewhere in between, I wrote this book for you as a parent.

Because my life has been so directed and inspired by my participation in sport—leading me from athlete to coach to sport psychologist to a parent of young athletes—I've been on every side of the arena when it comes to concerns, fears, expectations, and dreams. I know firsthand the joys, life lessons, physical develop-ment, social opportunity, and more that sports can bring into one's life. I also know the many challenges parents face in various arenas of athletics as they try to create the right balance for their child.

I have written this book to address the most common questions I've been asked as a professional who has worked with athletes, coaches, and parents. I hope it will give you valuable insight and encouragement in your quest to give your child a positive introduction to sports, whether you have a future Olympic champion, or a child who just loves to play.

1

INTRODUCTION
to
SPORTS

Making Good
Decisions

My parents enrolled me in soccer—my first organized sport—when I was five, after I had pestered them for at least a year. I had spent two years watching my older brother play sports, and it looked like so much fun running around kicking a ball, sliding in the grass and mud, and playing with a team of friends that I wanted the same opportunity. I had no real proof yet that I would be any good in a team sport or would enjoy my first experience, but at five years old that really wasn't on my mind. My focus was on having fun and doing something outside of school and the house. I was elated when I finally got my opportunity to play.

Perhaps your young child has expressed the same aspirations. Or, maybe you recall your first athletic experience and what spawned your interest to play, inspiring you to give your child the same opportunity. Whatever the motivation, you no doubt have questions about making the best decisions when it comes to introducing your child to a sport. The following answers to common questions will give you guidance to set you on the right path.

Q   Why should I allow my child to begin a sport?

A   Besides being a fun activity and an opportunity to get outside, interact with other kids, run around, and maybe even get dirty, sports or any athletic activity can also be an opportunity for children to learn and develop motor skills. Two of the more basic benefits of athletics are learning how the body functions and developing coordination skills. On top of that, emotions naturally develop with athletic participation and competition. Children are able to experience their bodies in different ways by feeling the rush of adrenaline and excitement as they anticipate an action, the surge of energy flowing through their muscles and joints while in action, the physical, mental, and emotional challenge of competing with others, and the feeling of satisfaction that comes with accomplishment and success.

Here is a brief list of what children can develop through participation in athletics:

1. Strong physical capabilities
2. Emotional awareness and understanding
3. Analytical reasoning
4. Decision-making skills
5. Leadership qualities
6. Personal responsibility skills

7. Team awareness and the ability to work as a team member
8. Communication skills
9. The ability to listen to and accept feedback
10. The ability to follow directions
11. An appreciation for time and time management
12. The effort and dedication needed to commit to achieving a goal

Q When should I allow my child to begin a sport?

A Introducing your child to sports at an early age (four to nine) is often a great way to support motor skill development, mental processing, problem solving, social awareness, and verbal and non-verbal communication skills. Some well-run sport programs can also teach or reinforce the positive values and character strengths that parents are providing at home. For example, martial arts teach structure, discipline, respect, patience, and self-control, along with fundamental and fine-tuned motor skills. All of these complement sound parenting.

As a parent, you may decide your youngster is ready to participate in sports; your child may likewise express interest in participating in organized sports, particularly if he has an older sibling already participating. You then have the opportunity to research the sport of interest, identify participating leagues or teams in your area, and find an appropriate program that teaches the fundamentals of the sport.

Q   Is there an ideal age to allow a child to begin playing a sport?

A   No. But some sports, like gymnastics or tennis, provide opportunities for younger athletes to excel at an earlier age, and there may be rewards for early acceleration in a sport. For one example, a seven-year-old tennis prodigy may attract the attention of a professional development coach, which may provide an opportunity to train at an elite academy with the chance of becoming a professional tennis player. So the early development of fundamental tennis skills may prove to be valuable. However, whether or not the child who begins playing tennis between the ages of four and six will become a prodigy by age seven depends on a number of variables, such as internal drive, commitment to training, access to tennis facilities and equipment, successful skills development, being the offspring of professional tennis players, or having passionate family members who encourage their children to play.

   In short, the ideal age to allow a child to begin playing a sport is when she is offered the opportunity and enthusiastically accepts, or when she expresses interest without prodding.

Q   Which sport should we choose?

A   The first sport you choose for your child is not as important as choosing the right program or coach. Select a program that has a strong commitment to teach the fundamentals of sport. So many introductory sport programs are focused on teaching sport-specific skills and finding the next great athlete that the necessary fundamentals are forgotten.

It's quite disturbing to read about or watch the countless stories of parents and coaches being enraged and becoming violent over youth sports; parents jockeying for their child to start or to get more playing time; or children being more concerned about the score, flashy sports gear, or jaw-dropping play to the extent that the core values, skills, and enjoyment of sport are lost.

So when you choose a sport for your child, also choose a program that is grounded in an educational philosophy to teach the fundamentals of play. Select a coach who is enthusiastic about teaching children how to attend to body awareness, the benefits of listening before talking, the amazement of successfully trying something new for the first time, and the excitement of building a new skill. Programs grounded in a fundamental teaching philosophy with coaches who enjoy teaching will most likely prove to be a positive first-time sport experience.

Q   Where do I find good athletic programs?

A   Community-based programs are a good place to begin. Local community centers, the YMCA and YWCA, and Boys and Girls Clubs of America rely on community participation, and they focus on the well-being and mind-body development of youth. Such programs with a mission to support youth development through positive programming can offer good introductions to sport.

Other opportunities to find a good athletic program may be through a word-of-mouth referral. For example, when you drop your child at day care, church, or school, have a conversation with other parents to find out about programs they have heard about or liked. The best athletic program for your child may be available in your neighborhood, but no matter where the program is offered, you'll want to ask the following questions:

- ❖ What is the program's teaching philosophy?
- ❖ How does the coach implement that philosophy?
- ❖ How many practices and competitions are scheduled?
- ❖ What does the program cost?
- ❖ Who is the coach and what is his/her sport or coaching background?
- ❖ Who will administer practices? If the coach will have assistants, what is their background in sport?

Be aware: the best athletic programs are not necessarily the most expensive or popular. A good athletic program should teach fundamental values and skills while fitting into your family schedule. For example, if the team you are considering for your child practices four nights a week, and you can only make one practice, the program is probably not a good fit.

Q   What if budget is an issue? Are there certain sports that cost less than others?

A   As I mentioned previously, the best sport programs or coaches are not always the most expensive. If you find a program that fits within your budget, you and your child will appreciate and enjoy the sport much more without the pressure of making payments or not being able to afford all of the equipment, participation fees, or facility dues.

There are sports that don't cost as much as others, such as those that don't require a lot of equipment or have facility fees or dues. Some lower-cost sports that provide excellent experiences are:

* basketball
* soccer
* swimming
* track and field
* wrestling

At an entry level, these sports require very little equipment and nominal to no facility dues. Today, most sport programs will ask for a participation fee, which may be sponsored or waived with proof of need for assistance. If budget is an issue for you, it's important to know that city or community programs often allocate funds each year to help offset the cost of recreation programs for low-income households. Those who qualify may receive 50% of program fees up to their allotted household limit. Because the amount of funding and number of subsidy requests varies, the city may not be able to provide a specific income cutoff for applications; however, families with the lowest incomes may be granted subsidies first.

If you're concerned about making an investment up front, consider asking the coach if your child can practice a day or two to see if he is ready to commit before any financial investment is made.

Q   Should my child already be good at sport before
       starting?

A   No, it's not necessary for her to already show talent—the
       point for most children beginning a sport is to learn about it
       and how to play. A good coach and program will ensure that
       each child is learning and developing fundamental skills to
       enhance her sport participation.

                          ❖   ❖   ❖

Q   What if my child wants me to coach or be actively
       involved in his sport?

A   Be thankful! If your child wants you to be actively involved
       in his sport experiences, it is a testament to your positive
       relationship with him and an opportunity to further develop
       that relationship. If you have some background experience,
       education, or training in sport, coaching can be a fun
       opportunity to demonstrate what you know, as long as your
       own competitiveness doesn't overshadow the teaching
       opportunities or the children's enjoyment of the sport. If
       you can stay focused on the kids and enjoy teaching,
       coaching may be a great opportunity for you.

           If coaching is not your calling, perhaps managing
       some aspect of the sport program suits you. Many youth
       sport teams need parents to coordinate team events,
       handle competition details, and plan banquets and awards.
       Last, but not least, every team needs a positive cheering
       section. Maybe that's the perfect role for you.

Going beyond being a supportive parent or coach—such as officiating or becoming involved in the governance of sport leagues—may be more about you than your child, so be sure your motives are sound. Simply put, if your child wants you to be actively engaged in his sport, make sure you're doing it for the right reasons—to benefit his growth and not your own childhood dreams or ego.

Q How do I choose a coach? Do I have any say as a parent?

A This is such an important topic. As a parent of a young child, you own the decision of choosing her coach, so you want to seek one who teaches and reinforces your family values. It's vital to give your beginning athlete the opportunity to learn how to be a sound individual of high integrity and character, while developing mind and body performance skills at the same time. Being present for the entire practice can help you determine if the coach is indeed a positive role model for your child.

A coach with integrity, good character, and who knows the fundamentals of movement and how to apply them to the sport will likely be a good coach. City- and community-based programs will almost always require a background check of any prospective coach, which should help you feel confident about leaving your child with an unknown individual. These programs will also likely provide basic coaching strategies, such as positive coaching, fundamental sport-specific information (e.g., program rules and regulations, player/parent/coach behavior expectations, training and competition schedule) and foundational training suggestions (e.g., warmup, practice suggestions, examples for specific training skills). These fundamentals, combined with a person of positive character and integrity, can offer you and your child a good experience.

The following is an example of how a good coach may begin a practice.

He starts by talking with the children and providing a structured approach to how they will learn to play the sport, demonstrating how positive communication and relationships can be established in a respectful manner while introducing sound performance skills. It may sound something like this:

"Welcome to softball! My name is coach Edwards. It's good to see some familiar faces, and I'm excited to meet those of you who are new to softball. I've coached youth softball in this league for the past six years and look forward to another fun season. Before we get started, let's go around the group so each of you can introduce yourself. Please say your name and if you've played on a softball team before. Talk loudly so we all can hear you. [children introduce themselves] Thank you! I'm looking forward to getting to know each of you better as the season moves forward. While we learn to play the game of softball, here are a few things that will allow us to have even more fun.

1. Bring a positive attitude.
2. Give your best effort.
3. Everyone stops and listens when the coach or a teammate is talking.
4. Enjoy the game!

If we all agree to these four rules, we will have a great time and a fun season!"

As a parent, you want a coach who makes the effort to connect with your child, so she feels welcome and a part of the team. From there, you want a coach who teaches through active engagement and interactive communication while kids are training. A coach who teaches a young softball player sound conditioning drills that include proper running technique, core strength, eye-hand coordination, bat-to-ball, and ball-in-glove coordination is offering fundamental skills that will enhance a young athlete's general performance and softball-specific skills. While these skills are being introduced, a coach who provides feedback in the moment through descriptive communication (e.g., "See the ball into your glove and secure it!") or demonstration (e.g., proper running technique drills) is strengthening the learning process.

On the other hand, if the coach of, say, your child's basketball team is diagraming a pick-and-roll screen as part of the triangle offense during the first practice, your kid will most likely be staring at the ceiling, confused, and on the way to losing interest. Consider also the martial arts coach who finishes a pleasant introduction to the kids and parents, but during training becomes a "screamer," berating the kids for poor performances and lack of attention to detail. Again, it's important to be present for entire practices when you're able. The actions of some coaches may discourage you and your child from continuing with their program, but hopefully not turn you away from sport altogether.

A USA Track & Field athlete I worked with for many years had the experience of training with a variety of coaches. She described wanting a coach who was similar to her parent—supportive and encouraging—expecting him or her to fill a similar role. No matter how successful or well regarded, coaches who used yelling and negative reinforcement to motivate did not work for her; supportive coaches who taught using positive reinforcement worked best. As many athletes do, she excelled with those coaches who identified and developed her personal strengths as well as her athletic abilities. You will likely find that your child is motivated by the same.

As you research sport programs and coaches, don't be afraid to ask specific and detailed questions. You want to learn as much as you can about the individual(s) who coach your child so you can feel at ease leaving him or her under their supervision. For example, when enrolling your child in school, you want to know:

❖ who will be teaching the class
❖ the teacher's background and educational experiences
❖ how the teacher maintains order and discipline in the class
❖ how the teacher manages unruly or defiant students
❖ what positive reinforcements are provided to encourage student learning

Selecting a coach is not much different and should be approached with similar curiosity and questioning.

Q   What if I can't make it to practices or games?

A   Many people keep a hyperactive pace that already involves juggling work, school, family, friends, and socializing.

Therefore, it can be a challenge when your child wants to get involved in an extracurricular activity like sports. Between the practices and competitions alone, there will be additional time and resource commitments on top of what you currently juggle.

Sometimes you may not be able to make a practice or game because of other work, life, and family needs; however, when you prioritize your child, making time to enjoy his development through sport will become an unwavering commitment you will happily make. When you do, you will have the opportunity to see your child grow mentally, emotionally, and physically as he learns through new experiences.

It's crucial that you take the time to review the team practice and competition schedule prior to making a commitment. If your child is excited about playing and being part of a new athletic experience and team, and then you say you can't take him to practice or to a game, he will not only be hurt, but you will compromise the team as well. At the beginning of the season, put practices and games on your work and personal calendars to ensure you and your child will be able to enjoy the sport together.

While parental involvement is important for your child, if you can't be there for some reason, another family member, friend, or team parent can be a close second. Talk with your child about any absences you may have from a practice or competition and who will be there in your place. Let him know who he will see on the sideline for reassurance, encouragement, support, or to share a celebration.

Q   What's an appropriate weekly commitment to sport at this age?

A   If you're concerned about how much time your child is spending in sport, here are a few things to consider.

First, every child, whether participating in sport or not, should enjoy at least one hour of daily physical activity. If your child's school provides recess or free activity time, it likely will not offer a full hour, so there is an opportunity to provide additional extracurricular outlets through sport.

Second, if your child participates in sport at an entry level, practices will likely be scheduled once or twice a week for an hour, with additional time for weekly competitions, which will vary depending on the sport. For example, a youth basketball game with eight-minute quarters on a running clock may take 35 to 40 minutes. A swim or track and field meet may last all day, particularly if your child competes in more than one event and advances to a semi-final or final competition.

Third, children who participate regularly in sport benefit more than those who give little or no time. Why? Because the more time a child spends participating in sport, the greater opportunity she has to enhance:

* her personal, team, and social awareness
* understanding of sport
* acuity for strategic thinking
* development and mastery of performance skills

All of these mental, emotional, and physical characteristics of personal development are beneficial not just in sport, but in academic performance and future career development as well.

In sum, the appropriate amount of time your child should spend in sport is dependent upon the amount of enjoyment and growth your child and family are receiving by engaging in it. You will likely find that the greater your commitment, the more pleasure and positive rewards you receive.

Q   What's the best way for me to prepare my young child for the commitment to and/or sacrifice of sport?

A   To ask this question about a young child interested in playing sports suggests that you are overanalyzing the simplicity of play. Allow your child to play freely and engage in a fun activity without being over-talked, over-prepared, or psyched-up. Your son or daughter is a child— allow him or her to learn how to adapt to schedule changes, new activities, developing friendships, learning new skills, or communicating with a coach.

A better question to ask is:

> "How should I prepare myself for my child's commitment to sport?"

Begin by remembering that your child has the opportunity to discover his or her own interests. As a parent, you can and should be part of the decision, but let your child decide which sport he or she likes. Here are some ways you can achieve that:

- ❖ Play freely with your child.
- ❖ Introduce a variety of sports to him or her.
- ❖ Attend sporting events together.
- ❖ Read about sports with your child.

Q   What's a good goal for my child in sport at this age?

A   Remember, we are introducing your child to sport so he will enjoy a healthy and happy experience. A young child's interest or understanding of goal setting and accomplishment is not as important as having fun learning.

You should have a similar goal as a parent (to have fun!), with the responsibility of ensuring that your child is doing the same. And if you need some guidance, the S.M.A.R.T. method is always a good one to focus on to help you enjoy your child's sport experiences. Keep your goals:

❖ **Specific** – Clearly define the what, where, when, why, and how you will accomplish your projected goal with unambiguous details.
   Example: Enjoy teaching and playing different sports with my son.

❖ **Measurable** – Set quantifiable markers to keep track of your progress and to alert you of goal achievement.
   Example: Dedicate a couple days a week after work to teaching and playing the fundamentals of sport with my son.

❖ **Actionable** – Include action steps that need to be taken to achieve your goal.
   Example: Learn how to enjoy teaching the fundamental skills of agility, balance, and coordination.

❖ **Realistic** – Set a goal that is a bit of a stretch, yet within your reach.
   Example: Introduce how the fundamentals of agility, balance, and coordination can be used in different sports.

❖ **Time-Bound** – Establish a deadline for when you will achieve your goal.
Example: Dedicate two days a week for one month to teach and play with my son.

S.M.A.R.T. Goal Example: Next month, I will dedicate Tuesdays and Fridays before dinner to enjoy thirty minutes of teaching my son the fundamentals of agility, balance, and coordination while playing different sports.

Q Should I make a deal with my child about trying vs. quitting before beginning? Should she be expected to finish the commitment once started?

A When you and your child decide to participate in a sport, you should also decide to make a commitment to complete the season, without bargaining or dealing. It's a great opportunity to teach your child how to follow the motto, "Finish what you start." Through the course of the season, you and/or your child may experience challenges with the sport, coach, practice, or competition schedule, or even other players or parents. Together, you and your child can talk about how you will work through the challenges and positively address moving forward.

Having said that, I know there are situations beyond one's control that make it impossible to finish what you started. If there are unforeseen and uncontrollable circumstances that diminish the value and enjoyment of playing a sport, or that create a detrimental environment, these are reasons to walk away. However, a loss, poor performance, being challenged, or not being selected are not good reasons to quit. Discuss with your child her thoughts about quitting, alternatives to quitting, ways to follow through, and next steps. Also consider getting outside help. Coaches and other parents may be able to provide a different perspective.

My grandparents always got a great kick out of telling a story about how competitive I was, even at an early age.

Every summer, my older brother and I would visit my grandparents on their farm in Blythe, California. After doing chores in the early hours of the day before the sweltering heat became unbearable, my brother and I would go inside to have lunch and to play with my grandparents. Checkers and dominoes were family favorites. One afternoon, the four of us were playing dominoes. I was scoring points and enjoying the game; I always played to win. When I didn't, I would ask to play again and again until I was victorious. Well, I guess with this particular game, either I wasn't playing so well, or my grandfather—who was a very good strategist and a math wizard—was really playing to win. At one point in the game, my grandfather scored big and I got upset, so much so that I wiped all of the dominoes off the table onto the floor and grumbled, "I hate this silly game!" My brother was upset because I had ruined the game. But my grandparents— without hesitation—laughed, calmly helped me pick up the dominoes, and encouraged me to keep playing. Reluctantly, I played another game, and another, and another, until I finally beat my grandfather.

I appreciated my grandparents for not letting me pout like a sore loser and quit. Instead, they offered guidance and encouragement to help me learn persistence, experience new opportunities, and not fear a challenge. I've remembered and carried these lessons into who I am as an athlete, parent, coach, and sport psychologist.

2

SPORT
CULTURE

Camaraderie,
Coaching & Commitment

As a kid, athletics were fun for me; playing sports was a great way to stay outside, play with friends, laugh out loud, yell, be aggressive, and compete—all of the things that were discouraged in the classroom. Athletics also provided the release of physical and emotional energies, as well as a chance to build relationships with coaches and teammates. Perhaps you, hopefully in the best of ways, experienced the same.

Building relationships with teammates and coaches will have ups and downs. You will find that events outside of sport may sometimes need to take a back seat, requiring you to excuse yourself and your child from attending. I learned early that my participation in sports required commitment and at times restricted me from experiencing other potentially fun activities. In fact, I missed my college graduation ceremony to compete in the

US Track and Field Outdoor Nationals. As a parent and coach, I likewise have missed after-school events, celebrations with family and friends, and career opportunities because of a commitment to my child's athletic activities or my coaching responsibilities.

Bottom line: you and your child will definitely have to make sacrifices when you participate in sport. At times those sacrifices can create ambivalent feelings, which may cause you and your child to question your decision to participate. As ambivalence increases, you will need greater self-motivation to continue the commitment.

Before your child signs up for a sport, I strongly recommend taking the time to identify what kind of experience you want your child to have, as well as the personal values you want emphasized in a chosen sport, and use the opportunity to create an enjoyable environment for your child. To navigate some of the trickier situations that may arise, the following are answers to common questions I have encountered.

Q   My child doesn't seem to fit in or is excluded from the social interaction among the team. What can I do?

A   At any age, developing a connection with sport can be compared to developing friendships, as both are based on a feeling of connection or acceptance. For example, a child's first day in a new classroom may be scary or uncomfortable because every face is unfamiliar and there is no recognized routine to follow. It may not be until the child connects with another student through conversation or a game that her defenses are lowered and she feels more comfortable with the new environment. As her comfort increases, her feeling of acceptance does as well, allowing friendships to be forged—often within group activities where she's able to identify shared interests or desires with other children.

Athletics provide a similar environment. Friendships created in an athletic setting may begin for children who share something in common, such as the same physical activities, motor skill development, or motivation to achieve. If your child doesn't connect in this way with anyone, offer her different approaches to communicate her likes and dislikes, or to ask engaging questions or make comments that draw her closer to her peers and coach.

Here's an illustration:

> Jordan feels bullied by other athletes on the team who are more aggressive and push her out of the way during exercises. As a parent, you can help her recognize that kids are having fun playing and may not realize they are excluding or making her uncomfortable. You may help her develop a positive phrase or statement to use when she feels uncomfortable with the other children such as:
>
> "You're really good at this! Can I try?"

It is important to allow your child to learn through experience. If she continues to feel out of place or is excluded, consider alternative options such as speaking to the coach about making inclusion a priority with the kids, or by having a meeting with the parties in conflict to proactively address the issue(s) and move forward.

Q My child is more focused on being social with his teammates than playing the sport. Is this okay?

A At this early age and stage of sport participation, children are very likely to be enamored with the new social experiences that come with playing a sport. For your child, the athletic environment can be similar to a school social, where he suddenly recognizes a competitor as a classmate and friend. Before you know it, the competition venue has become another social opportunity for friends to talk and laugh about whatever they find entertaining.

There are many opportunities for a young athlete to get lost in being social. Often, positive redirection on how your child can perform is enough to refocus him on the sport, such as, "You'll have plenty of time to talk and play with friends after the game. Right now, enjoy playing the sport together."

Q   **What if the coach and I don't get along?**

A   This all depends on why you and the coach don't get along. If your issue has nothing to do with how your child is currently being coached, it can negatively affect your child's opportunity for a positive athletic experience. Your child is participating in the sport, not you; remember to keep her best interest as your priority. If your child is having fun, enjoying the athletic experience, making friends, and learning, you may need to put aside your personal feelings or conflicts. Refocus on your child, how she is performing, and how you can support and encourage her efforts.

If, however, you disagree with how the coach is instructing your child, and you believe his/her approach is having a negative impact, I suggest you find a neutral time —such as before or after a practice—to talk with the coach privately about your concerns. After a short conversation, you may discover that your issue is a simple misunderstanding, or that by working together you can agree on a reasonable adjustment to his/her approach that allows you and your child to continue enjoying the sport.

Lastly, consider listening and taking in as much information as you can before voicing concerns. If necessary, use a third party to facilitate or even mediate a discussion between you and the coach. Bottom line: Make sure your conflict does not become your child's conflict.

Q **What if the coach is more competitive than my child and I are?**

A This will hinge on whether or not a more competitive athletic environment is right for your child. Having a more competitive coach may challenge or create new opportunities for your child to enjoy and grow in sport, rather than be the detriment you perceive.

For example, some kids disengage or become bored with sport because they're not challenged. A competitive coach can engage kids through stimulating exercises, drills, skill developments, and competition. If, however, your child isn't responding well to a competitive coach, consider these options:

- ❖ working with the coach to communicate in a less competitive manner with your child
- ❖ talking with your child about how to manage his reactions to more competitive people by refocusing on his personal strengths and abilities
- ❖ looking for another less competitive athletic opportunity

Personally and professionally, I have found that the second option works very well to redirect attention from what's undesirable to what's manageable. A positive method to stay focused and not be distracted by something undesirable is to give your attention to what is within your control. When you perceive something or someone demanding more than you can manage—which defines stress—a great way to manage that stress is to simplify your focus. Your child may find it helpful to do this by focusing on a manageable task, or a task that he does well.

I once talked with parents about their concerns regarding a high school coach who was so competitive that he became more negative than positive in his quest to win. The coach berated players with negative feedback, derisive comments, and foul language. A few kids quit the team as a result of the coach's behavior. The remaining kids and parents were upset and tried to find a way to help the coach and improve the program.

When a parent called and explained the situation to me, I asked how the kids were making it through practice. I was told that they didn't say anything until they left practice and then complained to each other and to their families. I was also told that the kids made faces to each other during practice, rolled their eyes, and played without spirit or intensity.

Right away I saw an opportunity to refocus attention away from all of the negativity and back to sport performance. I asked one parent why his child continued to play the game, and he quickly responded by saying his child loved the game and would never quit. Knowing that the player still enjoyed the game was a positive sign. I asked the parent to encourage his child to practice with intensity no matter what, making every effort to respond positively to the coach's performance requests. With a love for the game and a motivation to play, by refocusing on positive effort and behaviors, the player redirected attention from the unwanted verbal abuse to the desired positive performance. A week later, the parent called to tell me the complaining stopped, the players were talking and laughing about practices again, and there was a positive energy with improved performances.

Q Is it okay for me to talk with the coach if I disagree with what is being taught?

A Of course it's okay. But how, when, where, and why you disagree with the coach needs to be carefully determined. Not every youth coach may have a coaching certification or even experience in that sport. Often coaches volunteer to support their own children or to meet a community need. If you have experience in a sport and disagree with what a coach is teaching, there may be an opportunity for you to ask the coach if you can help out. Offer suggestions, provide examples, or even demonstrate positive alternatives. These can all be helpful and yet not threatening to a coach. Be mindful not to let your ego, desire to show up the coach, or need to impress your child get in the way of providing positive instruction.

Find a time and place outside of practice and games to talk with the coach about your ideas or interest in helping. Remember the coach made the commitment and likely went through the community requirements and background checks to take on the responsibility; your child and her teammates are being taught to recognize the coach as a responsible authority figure. Thus, show your respect for the coach's position and commitment by communicating your ideas in a respectful way that can be heard with an open mind.

❖   ❖   ❖

Q   The coach really doesn't teach; he/she only practices certain skills. Is that okay for my child at this age?

A   At this early stage, practice should incorporate a lot of fundamental skills building and teaching through play. Children will benefit from learning the A-B-C's—or skills of agility, balance, and coordination—and how these skills can be applied to the sport. Exercises, drills, games, and competitions can be used to accomplish this.

Here are a few examples:

❖   Warming up with exercises like 50-meter strides teach the proper running positions and technical form.

❖   Doing jumping jacks and burpees teach agility, balance, and coordination.

❖   Playing games like "Simon Says" or "Get Like Me" with different sport-specific skills teach the A-B-C's.

❖   Gymnasts practicing a jump routine on the beam 10 times gives the challenge of placing the feet in the exact same spot all 10 times.

❖   A soccer team practicing moving the ball down field to take a shot on goal without losing the ball teaches technique.

There is value in practicing. In individual and team sports, learning takes place during moments of play. Athletes learn to experiment with what works and what doesn't; they also learn to think critically, adjust current techniques, find new approaches, and develop successful skills during play. What's more, they learn self-awareness, successful communication skills, and how to manage their emotions—all during play.

Q The coach pays attention to the "star" players, not mine. How do I approach the coach about this?

A Continue to support your child's interest in sport and development by asking what he wants out of his participation. Maybe he is fine with not receiving direct attention or feedback from the coach—your child may be a residual learner who prefers to manage the anxiety or pressure of learning by watching others receive instruction. In short, your child may be comfortable with his experience.

However, if your child wants and needs feedback from the coach and is not receiving it, there is an opportunity for him to develop his communication skills and ask the coach for direct feedback.

For example, a child who feels he is being overlooked by the coach can use time before practice, during a break in training, or directly after practice to ask the coach what he can improve upon. He can then follow up, asking the coach what specific skills (e.g., endurance, strength, speed, ball skills, team plays) he can develop that the coach can evaluate during practice and provide him with feedback.

Building a line of communication with the coach using tangible S.M.A.R.T. (Specific, Measurable, Actionable, Realistic, Time-bound) performance goals can help your child get the coach's attention and direct a clear channel for what can be communicated to help him succeed.

Q My child complains about going to practice/ competition. Should I be concerned?

A If it is unusual for your child to complain about practice, it's likely a clue that something is different—but different doesn't necessarily mean something is wrong. Explore what occurred throughout the day prior to and after practice, as well as what's going on at practice and any significant changes. Your child's response may explain why he is complaining.

For example, your child—who really enjoys playing baseball—comes home and complains about not wanting to go to practice because it's too hard. His reaction may be the result of the coach redirecting or disciplining him in front of the team for not following directions or not hustling during practice, making a point that no individual on the team is above the rules. Your concern may need to be directed toward how your child reacts to responsibility, responds to direction from the coach, and returns to practice/competition.

In another scenario, your child complains about going to karate later in the evening, after you get off work. She tells you she wants to go to the earlier class and asks if you can leave work earlier. You may be concerned because going to the later class had not been a problem in the past; however, your child may be indirectly asking you to spend more time with her and less at work. Changing your work schedule, if it's an option, may be a way to address your child's desire to spend more time with you.

Conversely, you may notice while watching the class that your child is practicing with older kids and may be afraid of testing her skills against older, bigger students. In this case, your child's fear of injury and embarrassment are causes for your concern and should be addressed. Talking with your child and the instructor about how your child can manage anxiety and fear will help, if she continues to practice with older, bigger students.

Developing relaxation exercises, using positive thoughts to reframe perceived obstacles into manageable opportunities, and focusing on personal strengths to help execute skills successfully will also assist your child and address your concerns (see Appendices A through D). Otherwise, if the disparity in age and size are a detriment to your child's learning, switching to a more appropriate class may be the best option.

Q What if my child wants to quit before the season is over?

A If your child suddenly announces he wants to quit, definitely ask for and listen to the reason. Is this just an outburst sparked by momentary frustration, or did something significant happen in practice or competition?

For example, if the coach disciplined your child at practice and he was embarrassed in front of his friends and teammates, you can help him see that it was an isolated incident he can learn from. But if he feels threatened or unsafe, or if he realizes his ability has peaked and the sport is no longer a positive outlet or provides a feeling of accomplishment, then you definitely want to listen and offer support to help him make a decision. Being listened to and feeling accepted may be the support he is seeking and hasn't found in a coach or teammate.

Many times, the "I want to quit" outburst is just that—an outburst and nothing more. There is often no real desire to leave a sport that is providing a pleasurable outlet and a feeling of accomplishment. Your child may simply be asking for your attention, so be sure to offer it.

As I discussed in Chapter 1 on the topic of quitting, I prefer to heed the "finish what you start" motto, but I also know there are sometimes situations beyond one's control that prevent being able to finish everything we begin. Again, if there are unforeseen and uncontrollable circumstances that diminish the value and enjoyment of a sport or create a detrimental environment for your child, then it's time to walk away. However, a loss, poor performance, being challenged, or not being selected are not examples of reasons to quit.

I recommend discussing thoughts about quitting, alternatives to quitting, ideas for follow through, and next steps with family and your support network. This discussion can provide your child with different perspectives and approaches to making a good decision.

Q   When should my child commit to one sport?

A   There may be a push in America to commit children to one sport by middle school so they can be scouted by college and professional recruiters. However, in my experiences with youth, high school, college, Olympic, and professional athletes, there is a wide age range for when successful athletes commit to their sport. I have witnessed more unhappiness, injury, and burnout in athletes and families who committed to a sport at a young age.

There is and will be only one Tiger Woods. Not every child is going to pick up a golf club at age two, maintain the drive, focus, and commitment to master the necessary sport-specific skills, and years later become the number one golfer in the world. Through our mental, emotional, and physical development years, we need to build fundamental skills of:

- body awareness
- agility
- balance
- coordination

- internal motivation
- balanced muscle memory
- self-awareness

- communication
- self-esteem
- appropriate social skills

These will develop by engaging in a variety of individual and team sports. For this reason, I encourage parents and young athletes to play and enjoy a range of sports if they can, as long as they can.

As someone with an extensive sport background and three young boys of my own, I encourage and enroll them in individual sports like tae kwon do and track and field, and team sports like soccer, basketball, and baseball to offer them a variety of learning and growth opportunities. My boys also enjoy free play with friends in the neighborhood, as well as diverse social and learning experiences to enable growth in self-awareness and social strengths. I'm confident that this diversity will transfer into positive sport performance.

If your child is already passionate about pursuing an athletic career in college or beyond and exhibits the abilities to compete at a higher level, she will most likely self-select which sport to commit to and when that will happen. Feedback from parents, coaches, mentors, and friends can support your child's decision.

Q   If my child is terrible and hates the sport and wants to play a different one, is it appropriate to let him quit and start another?

A   Children experimenting with their first athletic opportunities—and parents learning to identify what a child likes and dislikes—will likely face some unsuccessful experiences. As a parent, you know your child best and have the clearest gauge of when and how far to positively push him to learn from new experiences. Parents who teach and instill fundamental values like integrity, trust, determination, and honesty may find that their children whine or complain on occasion about something new, challenging, or uncomfortable. But when parents establish and maintain clear sport boundaries (e.g., on-time attendance to all practices and competitions, responsibilities to manage equipment, respect for coaches and other athletes, positive performance effort) with limits for inappropriate behavior, their children push through new challenges and discomforts to experience new heights of achievement.

In the extreme case when your child simply doesn't like a sport, will not engage, and is not developing, it may be in your best interest to thank the coach and inform him/her that the sport is not working out for your child. You don't want your child to attach one negative sport experience with all sports, so if he really is not engaged in one athletic experience, introduce him to another enjoyable opportunity in a different sport. It's also possible that during the next season of the sport your child didn't like, he will have friends who are playing, or you may have identified a better coach. This can provide another opportunity for him to reconnect with the sport and perhaps have a different experience.

Growing up in Seattle, I lived near Lake Washington. On the occasional hot summer day, it would be fun to jump into the lake or go to a pool to swim, which meant I had to take swimming lessons. My mom and dad found a pool where my brother and I took lessons—and where my brother seemed to be a natural swimmer. He jumped in unafraid of the water, learned easily to float, and used different strokes to carry him from the shallow to the deep end of the pool. I, on the other hand, was not so adventurous in the water; I usually had a stomachache when it came time for swimming lessons. Sometimes those stomachaches prevented me from even getting into the water. My anxiety about being underwater and unable to float—let alone swim—was overwhelming.

When I got into the water, I felt like my goose-bumped flesh covered a metal skeleton. I struggled to stay parallel with the surface of the water. The more I struggled, the more I sank, and the more I wanted to exit the pool. My typically fast feet couldn't help me in the water. If only I had known then how to slow down my thoughts, control my breathing, and manage my anxiety (again, see Appendices A through D). I hated swimming! But twice a week my parents dressed me in my baggy swim trunks and sometimes needed to offer extra encouragement to get me to the pool. My fear of drowning and dislike for swimming was intense.

I remember the day we had to dive to the bottom of the pool to retrieve a spoon. There was no way I was going down there willingly, but after a lot of cajoling, I finally closed my eyes, put my head underwater, and pushed my body as far as I could toward the bottom of the pool. I may not have retrieved the spoon, but I learned that I could go underwater, come back up, and get back to the side of the pool safely. At the very least, I learned how to save myself in the pool. That summer, my parents didn't let me give up or give in to my fears. With their positive support and encouragement, I started the process of managing my fear of the water, and my appreciation for knowing how to swim blossomed.

3

DEVELOPING
SKILLS

Time, Talent
& Motivation

Children have many skills to learn, new experiences to explore, and goals to achieve. An exciting part of parenting young children involved in sports is to witness their experimentation and adventurous nature as they develop skills. The challenge for you as a parent is to positively motivate your child through these experiences, allowing him to move and develop at his own pace. It can be an exciting time as your child learns what natural skills he possesses and what skills need to be developed. Further, you will learn how your child interacts and socializes with other children, as well as works through challenges and discomforts. Playing an active role in your child's athletic development is vital to his motivation, learning, skill maturation, performance, and enjoyment of sport. Let's explore how you can best accomplish that.

Q   How much time should we devote to practicing
    outside of the scheduled practice?

A   When children first begin playing, the scheduled practices
    are usually enough. If, however, your child wishes to
    practice more and you're able to devote the time to helping
    her develop her skills, just be sure the extra practice is
    quality instruction of correct skills, and to balance it with
    school and other activities.

Q   What if my child doesn't get to play?

A   There may be a number of reasons why kids don't get to
    play or compete. Consider the following:

   ❖   A child's skill level does not match the skills of
       other players or athletes in the sport.

   ❖   There are more athletes/players than
       opportunities or positions to compete.

   ❖   Without the parent's knowing, a child quietly tells
       the coach that he doesn't want to play in
       competitions.

   ❖   A child doesn't play well with others on the team.

   ❖   League rules prohibit athletes who don't attend
       practice from participating in games/
       competitions.

    The reason why your child isn't playing will help you
    determine if something needs to change.

❖ If his skills don't match those of other participating athletes, there's an opportunity for skill building with more practice, additional coaching, or one-on-one coaching.

❖ If there are more players than opportunities or positions to compete, again, this is an opportunity for a child to improve his skills and abilities in order to be recognized as an athlete who will impact performance.

❖ If there are other children not playing, there may be a chance to start another team.

❖ Sometimes children are just fine practicing a sport, but when it's time to compete in front of spectators, a perceived or real challenge—along with the knowledge that someone must win and someone must lose—may make children not want to compete. In these situations, it is not uncommon for a child to tell a coach he doesn't want to play—to the bewilderment of the parents.

❖ Sometimes, children have difficulty playing well with or against other children and are removed from play for their safety and the safety of others. For a child with poor behavior, playing time can be minimized and supportive redirection with positive reinforcement for improved behavior may be helpful.

❖ Finally, if/when children don't attend practice, some leagues will prohibit them from playing in games. Before signing up for a sport, parents should carefully check family schedules to make sure their children are able to attend practices and competitions, so as not to jeopardize their opportunity to play.

Q   What if my child isn't very good at the sport?

A   We hope that children beginning their athletic experiences are having fun and enjoying new opportunities to learn and challenge themselves. Any judgment, good or bad, about a child's performance is likely not created by the child. Your ability to support her decision to play sports, guide her interest and enthusiasm, and encourage positive play will outshine a judgment of your child's ability level. As such, I encourage you to avoid judging your child's performance; instead, focus on her development of new skills, a positive attitude toward sport, and/or interest in diverse experiences.

Understandably, sometimes children are told, overhear, or even feel they're not very good at something. Some children will be motivated and driven to improve in order to change the negative feelings attached to not performing well, while others will feel demoralized but continue to work at building skills to improve play. In still other cases, the child will not recover from the negativity of poor performance, and will therefore walk away from sport. Imagine if someone had told Serena Williams she was not very good compared to her sister Venus, and she had walked away from the game of tennis. What if Michael Jordan had not been motivated to improve his game after being cut from his high school basketball team? What if Shaun White had become so discouraged after an injury or being unable to perform a difficult skill that he stopped snowboarding?

You can use stories of famous athletes such as these to encourage your child to pursue personal interests and passions, as well as develop skills to meet new or uncomfortable opportunities on the field of play. Leave judgment to critics and focus on enjoying the activity.

Q   My child is developing more slowly than other kids.
     Should I be concerned?

A   Every individual has strengths and weaknesses that
     contribute to ebbs and flows in performance. For example,
     as a child progresses in training and moves from a baseline
     level of performance to a higher level, her performance
     will plateau to allow for integration of newly learned skills
     and recovery, depending on how she learns. Some children
     need more time to integrate what is being taught into how
     they learn a new skill, and how they apply it to practice or
     competition. Pushing a child to progress faster will often
     slow down integration and mastery of skills, as well as
     successful execution, because it adds pressure. While some
     excel under pressure, others respond to it with increased
     anxiety, irrational thinking, rigid muscles, poor execution,
     and a roller coaster of emotions—all of which result in
     poor performance.

     If your child is interested, you may ask the coach if she
     could meet a few minutes before and/or after practices for
     additional coaching. Extra one-on-one teaching with the
     coach can pay dividends by increasing a child's motivation
     to learn, understand, and apply what's being taught, develop
     skills, foster willingness to compete, and further enjoyment
     of the sport.

     Overall, it's fine if your athlete is progressing at a
     slower rate. Michael Jordan and Tom Brady are two famous
     individuals who have talked about their gradual develop-
     ment as athletes. I would say it has worked out pretty well
     for both of them!

Q   How can I help my child get better at his sport?

A   The same way you can help your child learn to read, write, or solve math problems, you can help him get better at his sport. Spend quality time with your child watching the sport, talking about it, and playing it. Similar to learning a new subject in school, when a child becomes disinterested, complains, or gets tired of sport, take a break. Allow your child to dictate his interest. If a spark is ignited, then spend time talking about, reading about, watching, or playing that sport with him. The idea is to help your young athlete's interest blossom. That will require encouragement and involvement on your part.

If the sport your child expresses interest in is not one you are familiar with, do your homework to learn about it and why your child finds it interesting enough to pursue. Learn different drills you can do with him at home or outside of practice to feed his interest and desire to get better.

My boys wanted to play little league baseball and knew that I didn't play organized baseball growing up, so they didn't think I knew much about the sport. So I did my research on how to coach little league baseball and what skills are taught to first-time players. To support what my boys were learning at practice and what they enjoyed most—batting—I bought a batting T and whiffle balls so they could practice at home. I also cut a hole in a tennis ball, connected it to a rope, and tied the rope to the ceiling of our garage so the hanging ball could be used for batting practice. It was a fun, creative task the boys and I enjoyed doing together, and it gave them a safe and positive outlet to work on batting and to release energy in our garage.

There are many constructive and positive ways you can support your child's desire to be better in his sport. But make sure you match your involvement and passion to your child's so you don't overwhelm him with your desires or intensity.

❖ ❖ ❖

Q

My spouse pushes our child to do extra training on days off. Is this too much for her at this age?

A

For young athletes, you must ask yourself if pushing a child to train is fulfilling the child's desires or the parent's. I'm unaware of any valid proof that extra training with parents or personal coaches will guarantee a child's future success in sport. Sure, Malcolm Gladwell theorized in his book, *Outliers: The Story of Success*, that the key to success in any field is to practice a specific task for a total of 10,000 hours. Gladwell's theory was based on a study conducted by psychologist Anders Ericsson, who argues that the secret to winning is giving your full concentration during "deliberate practice" in a well-designed training program with an expert coach. Ericsson explains that daydreaming defeats practice, and full attention to task development and ongoing mastery is required under the guidance of an expert coach. A parent taking his/her child to the park to get in two hours of extra training a day does not qualify.

During the 10th Annual Big Sky Sport Psychology Retreat, Dr. Brian Hainline, the National Collegiate Athletic Association's Chief Medical Officer, encouraged the development of an athlete's fundamental skills before putting him or her on the playing field, in order to reduce overuse injuries and assure peak development in college and beyond. Dr. Hainline stated that kids mimic adult behavior, but do not have the neuromuscular control to manage the same behavior. As much as parents may promote their child's early development and youth "star" status, Dr. Hainline cautioned against additional training at younger ages. Pushing a young child to train is more likely to dissuade the child from enjoying the sport, may lead to overuse injuries, and may cause him to develop unwanted, negative feelings about sport, which may result in avoiding the sport altogether.

I've been asked by parents to train their children who are preparing for or are currently playing a sport, one of whom was a father asking me to train his six-year-old son playing on two select athletic teams. This six-year-old would play up to four games in one weekend and practice twice during the week.

The father wanted me to get his son in better shape through conditioning once a week, sometimes right before his team practice. Once I met the child, he expressed a genuine desire to play, so we used our training sessions to support his interest. We addressed his mental and emotional approach to sport more than physical training, and we discussed his motivation to play, emotional reactions to training and competing, and how to pace himself for competition.

The above scenario made me wonder if the need for additional training was really to benefit the six-year-old child or support the dreams of a father who had his own athletic aspirations. In sum, you must ask yourself: How does additional training help, and for whom?

Q   My child is overweight/awkward/uncoordinated
and the kids laugh when she tries to play. How do I
handle this?

A   Help your child build and maintain self-esteem with
unwavering support for every positive effort she makes.
Encourage personal development. Your job as a parent is to
guide, support, and encourage your child. When she is
feeling awkward or unsure, support her strengths and guide
her through opportunities that encourage her growth.

An awkward child can also reap huge benefits when a
coach takes time to teach and develop the skills needed to
succeed in a sport. Then, merely being able to use those
skills in practice and competition can help a child's self-
esteem, as well as physical and emotional well-being. These
personal skills and others—such as positive communication, self-discipline, respect for self and others, and
emotional and energy management—can be gained by
participating in sport and will help kids feel comfortable in
their own skin, teaching them respect of individual
differences.

If you're watching your child's practices and don't think
the coach is aware of other kids laughing at or teasing her,
tell the coach about your concerns before the next practice.
Together, you can promote a safer and healthier playing
environment that focuses on reinforcing positive behavior.
The coach can make a rule that all player feedback must
reinforce a strength and uplift a teammate. This approach
will not single out any one player and will develop positive
communication, self-esteem, discipline, and respect for all
within the group.

Q   My child feels defeated because he isn't as good as the other kids. Is this ultimately hurting his self-esteem?

A   It's hard to see your child defeated, disappointed, sad, frustrated, or embarrassed. Sport will test your child's performance skills—as well as his emotional, mental, and physical skills—and as this occurs, differences in ability levels become more apparent. Competitive children will quickly assess whose skills are better, and because of this, coaches and parents have the responsibility to refocus a child's attention from comparing skills to building skills. The goal is to allow comparison to lead to positive, collaborative play that challenges each child to improve.

Sometimes, however, comparisons can lead to defeating, negative self-talk, frustration, or embarrassment. When this happens, redirect your child's attention to why he wants to participate in the sport, the strengths he possesses, and how he can use those strengths to be successful and have fun. Refocus your child's attention on his positive attributes, rebuild his self-awareness and self-esteem, reconnect to how personal strengths are applied to performance, and rejoice in what most likely will be an enjoyable performance.

A young track and field Olympian, who had already won a gold medal, came to see me because she was dejected and discouraged and was considering quitting her sport. She complained about a number of things, including injuries, not getting along with her coach, feeling family pressure to keep competing, and not performing the way she once had. After I listened to all of her complaints and gave her a recap of all I heard, I asked her what was the most troubling. In a soft voice, she said she felt that she could not keep up with other athletes. She reluctantly admitted how hard it was to say this out loud; after all, she was an Olympic gold medalist! But after years of success and competing on the biggest world stage as one of the best in the world, it was demoralizing to admit that she was afraid she was no longer as good as her competitors.

Of course, I saw the opportunity to let her know that she didn't have to be as good as everyone else; she only had to be as good as she could be. By redirecting her attention and motivation toward what was within her control, she began to change her focus to concentrate on her own skills and abilities. She agreed to stop following other athletes' performances and focus on her own development. She committed to setting daily goals for training, visualizing her successful performance multiple times before training, and integrating positive self-talk phrases into her day, such as: "Stay in my lane," "Focus on executing my strengths," and "Maximize this moment."

Gradually, she rebuilt her self-awareness to recognize when her thoughts were negatively affecting her perform-ance. She successfully used positive self-talk and visualization to rebuild self-esteem, and she improved her health through rehabilitative exercises until she was free of injuries and pain. She improved communication and her relationship with her coach, and she spoke with her family about her career choices and how they could be supportive. Her self-esteem and confidence returned. In training, she was able to reconnect her strengths to repeated successful perform-ances, and she began to enjoy competing again at the highest level. Eventually, she fulfilled her dream of winning another gold medal.

Q How can I motivate my child if she becomes bored or disinterested in the sport?

A Sport is meant to be a fun activity. If your child is becoming bored or disinterested in the sport, consider why she is no longer having fun. For instance, is the sport demanding so much of her that she is overwhelmed? Think about how you respond to feeling overwhelmed. Your child may be disinterested or disconnecting as a result of too much stimulation or demands that are too high. Simplifying the skills your child is learning may increase her interest and enjoyment. In addition, you might consider these questions:

- Does the sport challenge your child enough?
- Does it leave her standing in lines or sitting on the sideline waiting?

Young children perform well in sport programs that keep them engaged with a variety of activities and active recovery times. For example, a 60-minute basketball practice for kids six and seven years old may have many different drills, including teaching and practicing dribbling, shooting, and free-throw positions, to name a few.

Between drills, instead of having kids stand idly waiting for their turn in line, encourage them to:

- Cheer for the other kids performing the drill.
- Watch other players to learn how to perform the exercise correctly.
- Do conditioning exercises, such as push-ups, sit-ups, or jumping jacks.

If your child spends more time talking, socializing, and playing with other kids in the sport, she's normal! Part of youth sport is to learn and develop individual and group social skills. Your child may not be bored or disinterested, but simply having fun socializing while not actively engaged in the sport. As a parent, you can help her understand when socializing is appropriate and when her full attention is needed for learning the sport.

Another way to motivate your child is to spend time enjoying the sport together. Make time to read stories, articles, or press clippings about the sport; or watch it on television, through video recordings, or attend a live competition.

For example, if your child is playing youth field hockey, take him to a high school, college, Olympic, or professional field hockey game so he can see how much fun it is to play the sport. Pick up the newspaper or go online the next day to read the highlights and discuss memorable points. Remember, these can be easy methods to engage your child in a sport and allow both of you to have fun in the process. Your child will respond to your interest and excitement; however, be careful! If your personal love for a sport is so over the top that you don't recognize your child has checked out and moved on, this exercise will only increase your child's disinterest.

Overall, you want to positively encourage active participation in sport, provide enriching athletic experiences, and educate your child about what makes sport fun and how he can enjoy it.

Q　My child gets really frustrated with mistakes and poor performance. How can I help?

A　Start by identifying the source of frustration. Allow her to express what causes the negative emotions and find a way for her to "blow off steam." If it's an issue of making a mistake or not performing a skill well, you can help her see it as a learning opportunity. You can also emphasize her positive performances and the enjoyable feelings connected to them. In short, help her concentrate on skills, no matter how small, that she does well.

If your child is frustrated in sport, ask yourself if you are seeing similar frustration in other areas. How are you addressing difficulties at school, with friends and family, or in other extracurricular events? With a positive approach to building skills, she can be encouraged to tackle just about anything.

It's also important to note that your child's frustration may begin well before she makes a mistake in athletic performance. For example, a child who lives within clearly defined boundaries of right and wrong at home and school may already have a need to be in control and do the right thing. When placed in an athletic environment that has been sold as being a fun experience, a child may expect an opportunity to play without the restrictions of discipline or right and wrong performance. As a parent, this is where educating your child about the sport and how it is played before practices begin can be very helpful, so your child is not disappointed or upset. In these situations, the time you or a coach invests in teaching and developing fundamental skills will pay dividends later on—as a decrease in frustration and an increase in your child's understanding and confidence.

4

HEALTH
and
SAFETY

Nourishment, Gear
& Injuries

I spent the entire summer between my freshman and sophomore year of college getting up three days a week at five o'clock in the morning to do therapy and strengthening exercises for a debilitating injury. During the rehabilitation process, I strategically pushed myself. I also learned more about and committed to a healthy diet. Fast food hamburgers, tacos, pizza, and top ramen were not providing enough fuel, not to mention any nutrition. So I vowed to cook more meals with high amounts of protein, fresh meats, vegetables, and fruits, and I carried fresh and dried fruits when I was on campus all day to avoid energy plunges and cravings for fast foods or sweets. In short, it was a lesson in the importance of self-care that has never left me.

It is my hope that you and your child will never have to deal with the debilitating injury or tedious rehabilitation I faced. I therefore encourage you to take steps to make your child's experience with sports as safe and healthy as possible.

To prepare your child properly, you need to think about everything from a healthy diet to equipment to the people who support athletic performance, should the need arise (chiropractors, massage therapists, physicians, physical therapists, sport dietitians, sport psychologists). This chapter will help you make decisions and take actions aimed at protecting your child's health and safety, both in and out of sports.

Q   What should my child eat and/or drink before a practice or game/competition?

A   The body is a miraculous machine, and in order for it to move and function correctly, it needs a source of energy in the form of nutritious food and clean water. Adenosine triphosphate (ATP) is a chemical in the body used to transfer and store energy, and we obtain ATP from the food we eat. Before a practice or competition, the body needs food to create ATP as an energy source.

It is widely documented that breakfast is the best and most important meal of the day because it gets us off to a great start and provides sustainable energy—the kind needed for a high-level performance, whether in school, at work, or in sports—and it's vital to provide this every day for our children. Here are some of my favorites:

❖   Fresh fruit/green juices
❖   Fresh fruit and greens (spinach/kale) smoothies
❖   Lean chicken or turkey sausage

- Egg omelet with spinach, onions, tomato, peppers, and cheese
- Seasonal fruit bowl
- Oatmeal with fresh fruit
- Short stack of multigrain pancakes with lean chicken or turkey sausage
- Granola and yogurt with fresh fruit
- Purified water with lemon squeezed in

Depending on the type of activity, different foods are recommended to sustain the appropriate energy. For example:

- An endurance performance athlete (e.g., in distance running or swimming, soccer, baseball, cross-country skiing) should consume many complex carbohydrates like brown pastas, potatoes, or brown rice for a slow release of energy. Protein is also important and can be found in beans, peanut butter, lean meats, and healthy plant sources, such as spinach and kale.

- A more explosive athlete in a dynamic performance (e.g., sprinters, martial artists, basketball players, gymnasts) needs protein to build muscle, which in addition to the protein sources listed above, can be found in lean meats and chocolate milk. If your child is not interested in eating before or after performance, a great option is an eight- to twelve-ounce glass of chocolate milk—preferably a healthy nut milk, such as almond milk—30–45 minutes before and after performance.

Most importantly, our bodies are made up of about 75% water, so your child should drink plenty of purified water to keep the body hydrated.

❖   ❖   ❖

Q   Parents alternate bringing snacks for the players, but they often bring unhealthy food or drinks I don't feed my child. Is it rude to bring our own?

A   I have seen snack bags filled with processed foods, candy, and unhealthy sweets. I have also seen snack bags for six-year-olds that look more like an adult's lunch. Furthermore, sodas, sports drinks, and most processed juices are terribly unhealthy beverages, yet parents often bring them, not realizing they're full of detrimental sugars and chemicals. Because of this, I often provide recommendations for snack bags for the teams I coach. An example would be:

"When it's your turn to bring post-game snacks, please provide a small, healthy snack, not a meal. Snacks can include:

❖ sliced or chunked fresh fruit

❖ granola or protein-style bars

❖ yogurt (preferably Greek) with no high-fructose corn syrup

❖ kale chips

❖ bottled water (no soda, juices, or sports drinks, please)"

If a parent brings a snack you don't approve of, simply have your own snacks as a backup that will nourish your child and that she will enjoy.

Q Do I need to purchase all the gear available for the sport?

A You definitely want to purchase all of the gear that is pertinent to the sport so your child is well equipped, safe, and appropriately fitted to participate. If certain items aren't required or necessary, a team manager or coach should be able to tell you.

For example, football players need the required and appropriately fitted helmet, protective pads, and shoes; purchasing the matching headbands, wristbands, towels, gloves, and bag, however, are likely not required.

Consult with the coach about what gear is necessary for participation and competition. Some equipment may not be needed for practice, but will be for competition. Running shoes, for example, may be required for track practice, whereas racing spikes may be required for meets. The parents of children who have past experience participating in the sport are also a great resource for sharing what equipment is necessary.

Q What if my child gets hurt?

A Your child can get hurt playing just about anywhere—at home, at school, with friends and family—and sport is, of course, no exception. Your reaction to your child's getting hurt may determine if he returns to whatever he was doing when the injury occurred. If your child gets hurt participating in a sport, allow him the opportunity to let you know if he wants to continue playing, take a break to recover, or stop playing or leave altogether.

While it may sound harsh, the truth is that getting hurt and recovering is a part of competition, as well as a great learning experience for you and your child. Be aware of how you respond to your child getting hurt and to how he responds to the pain. If you're a parent who quickly pulls your child from an experience as soon as he gets hurt, how will he learn to manage pain and develop skills to prevent future injury in that experience?

Think about this scenario: Your child gets kicked in the shin playing soccer and is lying on the field, crying. You rush onto the field, protectively scoop him into your arms, and carry him off to the bleachers to sit with you to recover and not play anymore. What has your child learned? That mommy or daddy will always be there to pick him up, take him away from bad feelings and experiences, and not have to deal with it as long as he cries long and loud enough. Is that really what you want to convey?

Give your child the opportunity to learn from manageable pain and how he can recover enough to continue playing. You and your child will become stronger, more adaptive, and more resilient as a result.

Having said that, this assumes you are able to determine between your child's being hurt and being injured. Early in your child's life, you probably witnessed the difference; if so, you can skip the rest of this response and move on to the next question and answer.

If you aren't sure of the difference between when your child is hurt or injured, consider this example:

Shaun is playing hockey in the street with friends. He has an open shot to the goal but gets pushed from behind and misses the shot while falling flat on the concrete. When he looks up to see the shot go wide of the goal and the other team change direction and score, he stays on the ground moaning and whining until someone comes to ask what's wrong. When the other players want to continue playing, Shaun is asked to continue as well. Once he realizes the other players are not sympathetic about the fall—and are not going to allow him to replay the turnover—his whining and moaning stop and play continues with no further mention of his mysterious injury.

This is a classic illustration of being hurt. There may be a physical "boo-boo"—with a little blood that can be treated with an ice pack for 20 minutes, or with a Band-Aid and a few minutes to rest and recover—but the hurt is more emotional and psychological trauma than physical pain. Shaun was upset about being pushed from behind and frustrated about missing the open shot. When play was not stopped to allow him to reclaim possession, he felt defeated and gave into the negative emotions, which resulted in being "hurt."

A true injury, on the other hand, would involve Shaun falling to the concrete and sustaining an acute trauma, which could include a laceration, contusion, ligament sprain, muscle strain, bone fracture, or head or spinal cord injury. In any of these unfortunate circumstances, he would need medical attention from a physician and would most likely require time away from competitive activity.

Q When is it okay to allow my child to play again after an injury?

A   If the injury is significant and she needs to leave a sport for a period of recovery, you should consult a medical provider about when it is appropriate for her to return to the sport. Sometimes injury can create hesitation or fear of resuming participation, so during recovery, make a point of talking to your child to make sure there's no fear about returning or feeling of pressure to meet someone else's expectations.

As a 19-year-old, I recall being hesitant and skeptical about returning to track and field after fracturing my right tibia. I had to relearn how to use my right leg, to trust that I could put pressure on it and not feel pain, and to rebuild muscle memory so I could walk again and eventually run. I remember questioning if the whole process was really going to work. It wasn't until I actually returned to a track and sprinted without pain that I felt reassured I could enjoy sports again. That's when I knew I had recovered and when I told my parents it was okay for me to return.

Considering how I felt at age 19, imagine how a young child might feel about playing a sport again following an injury. It's important for you as a parent to talk with your child about the injury, what she is feeling physically and emotionally, and what she can do to regain confidence after the injured area has healed. Children may not have the vocabulary to clearly express their thoughts and feelings, so activities can be helpful tools to encourage self-expression and build self-esteem and confidence.

For example, playing a game of Stop Light is a great way to help your child express pain. Red light describes a lot of pain and no interest to play, yellow light describes low to manageable pain with an interest and ability to play, and green light describes ready to play with no pain.

Depending on the extent of the injury, you may want to consult with a sport psychologist for additional suggestions on how to mentally and emotionally support your child and manage your own reactions to your child's recovery.

Q   **What if my child complains about aches and pains?**

A   Talk with your child about the specific aches and pains he is experiencing; he may be sore from the use of undeveloped muscles, experiencing a growth spurt, needing to recover from a performance, or seeking attention. During developmental years, it's not uncommon for children to experience soreness from use or overuse of muscles during practice. If their clothes aren't fitting properly and they're complaining about soreness, they're likely going through a growth spurt, which can be uncomfortable, if not a bit embarrassing, especially if the bottom of their pants stop just under the calf muscle.

If your child is going through conditioning or pre-season training, it is likely and expected that he's experiencing soreness. This activity is meant to establish a solid foundation on which to build strength and to refine performance skills. To establish a wide base, conditioning will challenge and expand your child's current fitness level, causing aches and pains in the process.

Also be aware that children may complain about aches and pains in order to receive attention. Make sure your child is not trying to tell you something about participating in the sport by complaining. For instance, he may use body soreness to get out of going to a practice that is challenging, that pushes him outside of his comfort zone, or that creates fear because his skills aren't fully developed.

On the opposite end of the spectrum, persistent complaining about aches and pains may signify that something is truly wrong. If your child continues to complain, contact your medical provider for an evaluation.

Q My child feigns or exaggerates minor injuries for attention. How do I deal with the drama and embarrassment?

A The truth is, the more attention you give feigned or exaggerated injuries, the longer the attention-seeking behavior will continue. It may be difficult and embarrassing to see and hear your child whine and complain about exaggerated injuries, but hold steady. Encourage your child to keep playing. Giving in to the drama by running to your child's rescue will only prolong the unwanted behavior. Allow the drama to play out. Once the scene has concluded, encourage her to continue participating and then celebrate the completed performance. Your child will learn that the attention she seeks can be received after successfully completing a performance (good or otherwise). Before long, she won't seek your attention during performance, and both of you can enjoy the sport.

PERFORMANCE
and
GAME DAY

Anxiety, Expectations & Support

For a young child, part of the fun of playing a sport is the adventure of discovering and learning new skills, so let your child dive in and experience sport with all of its expected and unexpected demands. Your guidance and support will provide him with a safety net, which your child will need even more if everything doesn't go as planned. Through the course of a season, your young athlete may face adversity from a minor setback—such as having a cold, a time conflict with a school event, or a planned family vacation—to a bigger obstacle, such as performance anxiety or a desire to quit. Through such adversity, you and your child will have the opportunity to learn the A-B-C's of performance, which will serve as a foundation for the topics of this chapter.

Q   What are the A-B-C's of performance?

A   The "A" stands for Awareness of self, skills and perform-
     ance, the "B" for Behavioral Adjustments to improve
     performance, and the "C" for Cue Words to enhance
     performance.

AWARENESS

Athletes have the opportunity to enhance self-awareness
through physical, mental, and emotional development.
Physically, athletes train to improve muscle coordination,
endurance, strength, flexibility, power, speed, and agility.
These physical attributes and personal improvements are
visible and can be measured to determine how well an
athlete is developing. Coaches and parents will be able to
see the changes, which presents the perfect opportunity to
motivate your young athlete.

   Give your child a "high five" to acknowledge and
support her progress. Past success and current progress are
terrific sources of motivation. Mentally, young athletes will
learn that how they think about sports can affect their desire
to participate, execution of performance skills, commitment
to compete, and overall enjoyment of their sport.

   To accomplish this, help your child practice two
techniques I often use in sport psychology: negative
thought-stopping and positive thinking with effective cue
words (see Appendices A & B). For example, a young
athlete who learns to use positive thinking will develop a
positive approach to training and will look forward to
participating with friends, building skills, and enjoying a
sport. As this young athlete matures and builds performance
skills, a coach will likely look to her as an athlete who sets

a positive example or as someone who is coachable. With developed cognitive and emotional awareness, such an individual will also be more able to distinguish between the varying emotions of happiness, excitement, anxiety, fear, frustration, and anger, which is a valuable key to having greater self-awareness.

BEHAVIORAL ADJUSTMENT

Increased self-awareness creates the opportunity to identify and adjust behavior to improve performance. How often does your child repeat the same undesirable behavior(s)? You can help him change his actions by showing him another type of conduct—or rather, a behavioral adjustment. Repeating the same or similar unwanted behavior may be due to a loss of motivation, lack of awareness, or lack of another behavioral option. You can point out the unwanted behavior to make the athlete more aware; however, the motivation to change the behavior may need a new behavior to stimulate change. To achieve this, provide positive alternatives to help your child adjust or to change unwanted behavior(s).

For example, consider a young athlete who is struggling to keep up with training workouts, loses confidence, is not connecting with teammates, and feels stuck and unsure of what to do. As a parent, you can take several steps to change this behavior, starting with acknowledging the athlete's difficulty, and encouraging him to talk about the workouts and what is going wrong. Next, praise the things he is doing well, and ask the coach about ways to help him have a better workout experience so he can improve performance. You can also reach out to other teammates to ask for their support. This approach gives the athlete:

 ❖ an opportunity to be heard
 ❖ a supportive outlet for his thoughts and emotions
 ❖ immediate feedback and connection with a
   supportive parent
 ❖ opportunity to connect with the coach and peers
 ❖ hope
 ❖ motivation not only to continue training, but also
   to pursue methods that can improve performance

CUE WORDS

We all have and use our internal voice to communicate likes
and dislikes, among other things. Our internal voice is a
powerful force that can talk us into or out of a great
performance. Allow the power of words to benefit your
child by creating and integrating meaningful words into
training and competition that inspire successful performance.

For example, an athlete who is often anxious before
competition may use cue words such as "breathe and focus"
to calm down and center herself in the moment. Cue words
can be powerful tools to manage thoughts and emotions
and to motivate athletes toward successful performances.
Music can also influence your child's performance. Many
athletes listen to music and recite lyrics as a source of
motivation. In fact, song lyrics can be used to develop
effective cue words in performance. Talk to your child about
the musical lyrics that inspire and move her to action. Cue
words can be powerful tools to manage thoughts and
emotions and to motivate athletes toward successful
performances.

When you incorporate the A-B-C's of performance into
your child's athletic experiences, you'll see the successful
outcomes in performance and game day execution.

Q How do I help my child when he gets nervous?

A Being nervous or anxious about performance is normal. Though we often misinterpret anxiety as negative, it can, in fact, be positive to support performance. So before you jump to the conclusion that nervousness indicates something is wrong, consider that your child may be excited by the anticipation of a positive performance.

It may sound strange, but there is such a thing as healthy stress—it's called eustress. Simply put, it is a positive cognitive response to an event, such as athletic performance, and the hope for a positive outcome. If your child describes thinking about a positive outcome to performance and being nervous to compete, he may be experiencing the positive effects of eustress.

On the other hand, when we are unable to manage the perceived challenge of an event or adapt to stress, we can experience distress. When a young athlete experiences this type of stress—which can manifest cognitively, emotionally, and physically—symptoms can include:

- dwelling on negative thoughts
- fears
- crying
- emotional outburst
- anger
- avoidance
- aggression
- passivity
- becoming physically ill

To help your child identify and manage anxiety, ask him the following questions:

- ❖ Why are you participating in the sport?
- ❖ What does participating in sport mean to you?
- ❖ What makes practice different from competition?
- ❖ Why is a specific performance important?

Within the answers lie the reasons your child gets nervous. Once you have a better perspective on what's creating the stressors, you and your child have a better opportunity to determine if he is experiencing eustress or distress, and how it can be addressed.

I once worked with a young soccer player who told me he got nervous before games against a rival team. Through a conversation about his team's style of playing soccer and his personal preference, I found out he prefers a finesse style of play. I asked him about the rival team's style of play, and he described them as playing a more aggressive style of soccer. He told me that he saw a teammate hurt his ankle after being tackled by a member of the opposing team, and his subsequent distress or fear was rooted in his perception that he could be injured like his teammate. He doubted his ability to manage the perceived threat of injury because he did not believe he could play well against more aggressive soccer players.

After discovering this, I positively pushed him to redirect his thoughts to the strengths of his own style of play and how he could successfully execute ball control and movement. We practiced using reinforced positive thoughts and performance cues to focus his attention on how he moved the ball well, and I immediately gave him positive feedback when he was successful. He described feeling secure in his abilities, reassured that he could play to his strengths, and confident that he could rely on his teammates. Emotionally, he described feeling secure, and he recommitted to playing his style of soccer. Ultimately, he reduced his fears and distress back to a manageable level of positive eustress, and he looked forward to testing his skills against more aggressive soccer players. As a result, he continued to play without fear, and he played well.

Kids may be nervous before new experiences or challenges. As a parent, you can reassure your child with positive discussions about how being nervous can mean he is excited and ready to play. Talk about why your child wants to play sports, what he enjoys about it, and how well he performs when having fun in the sport; you can then reinforce his strengths as an individual and as an athlete.

For additional tools to support a positive approach to managing nerves or anxiety, see Appendices A through F.

Q Should I treat a game or competition day differently?

A Sport participation for young children is meant to be a fun learning experience, whether it's a practice or a competition. Your positive approach as a parent should be no different for a practice or a game. Your child will react to your energy and emotion as much as, if not more, than your words.

For example, if you get excited about a Saturday competition, but struggle to get to weekday practices or can't wait to leave so you can get home or back to work, your child will sense that practice is not important or worth investing time and energy. So when you treat competition differently, think about the meaning you attach to your actions. Your child is watching.

When it comes to differentiating between training and competition, consider what your child gains from both. If she uses training to build and execute successful performance skills, competition will mimic training. Therefore, there is no reason to treat the day of competition any differently than a training day. That goes for the big competitions too.

From a performance perspective, the "big" competition is the same as any other contest that allowed your child to make it to the "big" stage. Sure, her emotions may be more intense, her thoughts may be focused on the desired outcome (which is good! See Appendix E for visualization techniques), and she may even be distracted by the hype that comes from making it to a championship round. However, your child can control that by managing emotions and thoughts, staying committed to the moment, and executing the skills she developed in training. As a parent, you want to enhance your child's enjoyment of the "big" competition, so be consistent in the attitude you display, whether it's in training or in a competition of any size.

Q   What if my child does well in practice but not on game/performance days?

A   When this scenario occurs, your child may be experiencing increased anxiety. Here are some signs to be aware of that may contribute to your child's increased anxiety and poor performance:

❖ PERCEIVED—AND EXPERIENCED—PRESSURE TO
PERFORM

("Will I live up to Mom's or Dad's expectations?")

❖ LOW SELF-ESTEEM

("I'm not very good.")

❖ FEAR

("If I perform well, people will expect me to
always be good." "If I don't perform well, people
will be disappointed or think I'm not good.")

❖ DISINTEREST IN COMPETITION

("I don't like competing against other kids. It's too
hard.")

❖ SOCIAL DISCOMFORT

("I don't like competing in front of people. I feel
like everyone is watching me. What if I make a
mistake?")

❖ FRUSTRATION

("I can't do it right! I hate this game!")

It is not uncommon to see changes in performance
from practice to competition. Some people are simply more
comfortable, alert, and relaxed during practice, allowing
performance to flow freely, but then approach competition
with increased tension, apprehension, doubt, and fear.
Often the meaning attached to practices and competitions
significantly affects performance. The difference is likely
contributing to your child's change in performance.

For instance, a child who is excited to run around with
friends, release energy, and play at practice likely enjoys the
freedom and fun of practice. When that same child
approaches competition and has a parent talk to him about

how to play the game the right way, be better than other kids, and do everything he can to win, he may become confused and anxious about playing. As his anxiety grows, he may focus more on what you've said than on enjoying the game.

It's important for children to have a positive introduction to enjoying sport without pressures or expectations for performance; attention should be placed on how they learn fundamentals in both practice and competition. This will protect children from unwanted mental or emotional burdens that will limit enjoyment and hinder performance. Parents should also attempt to maintain a consistent and equal emphasis on learning, building skills, and enjoying both practice and competition.

Q My child is inconsolable if she loses. How do I encourage a more positive outlook on winning vs. losing?

A As a young athlete, I envisioned my future athletic feats showing up on *ABC's Wide World of Sports* (ESPN had not been launched yet). However, I was often humbled by reality! What I dreamed about achieving for myself and enjoyed watching on television, I found difficult to duplicate. My performances did not always match my expectations, and I would get impatient and frustrated with my shortcomings. As much as I enjoyed celebrating my successes, I despised failure and tried to use it as motivation to avoid repeating poor performances. While not the best source of motivation, fear of failure definitely gave me the desire to work toward being successful.

Now, as a parent of young children with athletic aspirations—and recalling my own emotional outbursts after a disappointing performance—I find myself asking the same question about how to encourage a more positive outlook on winning vs. losing. From my experiences, I've learned and practiced how to redirect an athlete's attention from wins and losses to how he performs. When your child becomes inconsolable or emotionally upset, talk about the positive things in his performance: specific skills he used, skills that were executed successfully, or his effort to use a new skill. By engaging your child in a conversation that promotes positive thoughts, emotions, and behaviors, you can help change the way he views his performance. Discussing the process also keeps your child focused on his performance, which is where competitions are won or lost.

If your child continues to focus on the negative outcome and the win-loss column, try to find out what happened in the competition that led to feelings of disappointment, embarrassment, sadness, or failure. By understanding how he evaluates his performance, you may have an opportunity to explore approaches that can lead to achieving a more desirable outcome.

Here is an example of a young athlete who was inconsolable after a loss and her parents' subsequent interaction.

Sarah's soccer team lost the championship game. Still crying after the 20-minute drive home, her parents consoled her with hugs, kisses, and "I love you's," trying to reassure her that she'd have the opportunity to compete for a championship next season. Sarah, however, continued to cry. "But we lost and I did everything I could to win!"

Frustrated and puzzled about what to do, Sarah's parents allowed her to cry and share her thoughts and emotions.

They gave her support, encouragement, and unconditional love to help her accept the loss. But when Sarah continued to cry and seemed inconsolable, her parents decided to give Sarah space and time until she was all cried out. It also gave Sarah's parents time to calm down, manage their own emotions, and regroup.

Once Sarah was calm, her parents sat down with her to talk about how she played and how the team performed. With her emotions under control, and with her parents' encouragement, Sarah was able to talk about a number of things: the skills she performed well; what she could have done better; areas where her team could improve, as well as the great plays they made; surprising and memorable moments during the season; and thoughts about next season. The conversation helped Sarah move on and accept how her season ended.

Q
My child did something embarrassing during the competition and is now afraid to play again. What should I do?

A
Embarrassing moments are a part of sport as they are in life. I have experienced many—I know firsthand what it's like to wish you could have that moment back or change what made it embarrassing.

For your child, dwelling on the embarrassment will not change it or make it go away. However, encouraging him to acknowledge that the humiliation happened, take responsibility for his actions or inactions in that moment, and learn from the experience, will help him feel better.

If your child experiences an embarrassing moment while performing, encourage him to talk about exactly what was embarrassing. Then, talk through the following:

❖ What was within his control and what was not?

❖ How can he take responsibility to "own" his behavior?

❖ What could be done differently in the future to avoid embarrassment?

❖ And most important, help him accept the fact that perfection is not a human trait and move on.

One of my earliest and best sport memories was also one of my most embarrassing. You likely remember your first organized competition—the particular circumstances, the adrenaline rush, the emotions you felt. Mine was in track and field at the age of six, running a 50-yard dash.

I remember being given the smallest uniform the team had, and still it was way too big for me. I was a slender kid with an extremely small waist, and I remember my mom having me try on the uniform to see how it fit the Friday night before the meet. She probably used every safety pin in the house as she struggled to fit me into the tank top and shorts, folding, rolling, and pinning them to fit my small frame, all the while filling me with reassurance and confidence that I looked good. But I saw how much material those safety pins were holding and knew if I moved too quickly or squirmed too much, my shorts were sure to fall down and my tank top would fall off my thin shoulders. The next morning, my mom's tailoring skills and my running ability would be tested.

I was excited and scared about my first race as I thought about stepping out on the track and running in front of a grandstand of people. As I mustered the confidence to approach the starting line, trying to take my mind off how uncomfortable I felt, I remembered my mother's words of comfort: "You'll be fine. Have fun, Ross!"

There were many people watching, and I remember feeling incredibly small as I walked down the 100-meter straightaway to the 50-yard mark and stepped up to the starting line with seven other young sprinters, most of them between the ages of eight and ten. I recall looking down the track and seeing a thin string stretched across the finish line, identifying where we were supposed to stop. I then looked at the other kids I was running against and saw what I would now define as looks of fear, confusion, and discomfort. Then the gun went off and we were running.

After about 15 yards, I had the lead. I remember feeling the wind flying past my body and my uniform going with the wind—the folds, rolls, and pinning were coming undone! At 25 yards, I still had the lead but was losing my shorts. I had to improvise my running form to grab my shorts before they hit the track and the grandstand got a peak at my boyhood. But when I reached for my shorts, the pinned strap of my tank top fell off my shoulder. I ran the last 25 yards of my first competitive race holding onto my shorts and tugging at my shoulder straps to keep myself from being exposed. Believe it or not, I was able to reach the finish line in first place without showcasing my entire body. While it was embarrassing thinking of everyone—including my competition behind me—watching me clutch my clothes, winning my first race will always be an unforgettable moment.

Perhaps you have a similar memory you can share with your child to help ease the shame of feeling embarrassed. If not, feel free to use mine! I recall my parents laughing with me about that race, picturing me tugging at my clothes while I ran. For a while, I didn't like hearing my parents tell that story over and over and having everyone they told laugh at my expense. But I did appreciate those who recognized my ability to focus in the moment, not only to keep my clothes on, but also to continue running through the finish line. I learned to look at the positive outcome, how I adapted in the moment, and continued to compete. For those reasons, I actually came to enjoy sharing the story about my first race of athletic success!

Sport mirrors life. There are many valuable life lessons, including how to face challenges, how to learn and recover from them, and how to discover the unexpected opportunities a challenge may bring. Whether it's a last-second missed free throw that could have won the game, vomiting on home plate while at bat, scoring on your own goal in soccer, or losing your pants during a track race, your child can look at the incident as an opportunity to learn from the experience, improve so it doesn't happen again, and eventually talk about it as a funny memory.

Q   What can I do for my child the day of performance? (e.g., meals, snacks, packing her bag, etc.)

A   I always tell parents to prepare their young athletes for performance well before the day of competition arrives. Just as you prepare for a training day, have clothing, equipment, snacks, drinks, and travel arrangements organized, creating a stress-free environment.

A common phrase I use with athletes and coaches is:

Proper Planning Prepares Positive Performance.

When you have prepared a plan for competition day, you can enjoy it and more easily adapt to any changes that might occur. Your organization also provides a great example to your child for how to prepare for performance so that both you and your child can relish it.

Q

How much cheering from the stands is too much?

A

Encouraging your child with positive communication provides great rewards to her; however, there are limits. Overzealous parents cross the boundary when they take cheering onto the field of competition or into the personal space of others. I think most people recognize when someone's behavior becomes inappropriate. If you need examples of overenthusiastic cheering or obnoxious sideline coaching, there are plenty to watch on YouTube.

Talk with your child about how comfortable she is with your cheering and involvement. Some children don't want to see or hear their parents during a performance because it's a distraction, embarrassing, or too much pressure. Your child may be your best barometer of how much cheering or involvement is appropriate. If you need to tone down your verbal enthusiasm, so to speak, there are plenty of other ways to show your support for your child's participation in sport—such as a positive message on a sign, volunteering to help coordinate athletic events, working with other parents to help manage your child's team, or volunteering to coach.

Q   If I can't make it to a competition, how can I best
        show my support?

A   Understandably, there may be times when you are unable to
        make a performance. Do your best to find out in advance if
        you have any scheduling conflicts, then talk with your child
        about those dates or times that you won't be able to make
        the competition. Hopefully, you will have another family
        member, friend, or teammate's parent who can provide
        encouragement and support in your place. Having the
        conversation, demonstrating your disappointment about
        not being able to attend, and arranging for another person
        to be there offers your child the opportunity to see you take
        responsibility and show interest in his activities.

        You can also be there—without actually being there—
        with all of the available communication tools we have. You
        can arrange a time just before the competition or right after
        to place a phone call, send a message, or video chat to show
        your support. You could also work with your child before
        the competition to make a sign in support of him, then give
        the sign to whomever is taking your place at the
        competition. When he looks to the sideline and sees the
        sign, he will think of you and know you are cheering for
        him.

6

ROLE MODELS
and
COMPETITION

Positive and Negative Influences

People are often curious about where children get their ideas of athletic success. I can tell you that mine originated within my family—particularly from my maternal grandfather and my father —and were enhanced through my own athletic experiences and seeing other successful athletes in the newspaper and on television.

My maternal grandfather was a high school, college, and masters track star in Texas. My father was a high school basketball and baseball star, and a college basketball standout in Washington state. In addition to being athletically talented, both made significant contributions to their local communities and beyond— through education, community service, and politics. These two strong African-American male role models gave me clear examples of what it means to be driven, disciplined, responsible, accountable, independent, and a leader—characteristics I strove to incorporate and found to be valuable for athletic success.

Whether or not children are able to receive these valuable teachings at home, youth sport may offer an opportunity to find positive role models—much like a supportive and educational family system—providing leadership, guidance, nurturing, challenges, positive feedback, and redirection. This chapter will help to guide you on the topic of positive and negative influences.

Q My child looks up to a sports celebrity and wants to emulate him/her. Is that healthy at this age?

A I once coached a seven-year-old on a summer league basketball team who came to practice in a Kobe Bryant Los Angeles Lakers starter jersey, brand new purple and gold basketball shoes, and strap-on glasses like Kurt Rambis. His mom bragged that her son was extremely excited to play; he watched a lot of basketball on TV and memorized team and player statistics, and he was therefore ready!

Right away he peppered me with questions about his favorite team and player. Before I could answer completely, the youngster fired back that his favorite team was the Lakers, and Kobe Bryant was his favorite player. He continued to tell me about why he liked Kobe and how many Lakers games he had seen with his dad. He then asked to have the basketball I was holding. I passed him the ball and watched it ricochet off the palms of his hands, to his chest, knees, and feet, and then roll across the court. Once he reclaimed the ball, he ran it down court without dribbling, stood within five feet of the basketball hoop, and threw the ball three feet from the net. While the boy was excited about his opportunity to play a sport he loved to watch, his athleticism clearly didn't quite match his enthusiasm. But his passion was undeniable, and he was a pleasure to coach.

Children may aspire to be like a popular athlete their friends talk about, parents celebrate, and video games and TV highlight. Young children will emulate what they are exposed to, so when a child models a sports celebrity, it is likely because of the praise someone close to the child heaps on the athlete. As parents and adults, our responsibility is to point out positive personality characteristics and direct our children toward the athlete's strengths and away from the negativity our children may be attracted to in sport. If your child likes a celebrity sport figure, educate your child about what is healthy to mirror, such as his or her admirable characteristics, strong skills, positive family values, and commitment to community service. You can and should determine what is healthy for your child.

Here's a scenario to consider:

Let's say you and your child are watching a football game on television and he is excited to see a particular player who is getting a lot of media exposure. During the game, this athlete is involved in a series of arguments with opposing players, even shoving an official trying to break up one of his fights. Eventually, he is thrown out of the game. This type of event gives you a terrific opportunity to ask your child about what he has observed and what his reactions to it are. You may ask your child:

❖ "How do you think the coaches and teammates of the player feel now that an important member of their team has been thrown out of the game?"

❖ "How did the player's behavior affect the game?"

❖ "What would you do if you were a player in that game?"

❖ "What positive behaviors or steps could have been taken to continue playing the game and avoid such a poor outcome?"

❖ "What would you do differently?"

Your child's responses can open a great discussion about sportsmanship, respect for the game and those who play, and positive personal characteristics that can be taught and reinforced through sport. The conversation will allow you to learn about your child's understanding of these qualities, and at the same time teach him desirable personal and performance characteristics, without disparaging his athletic role model. With this kind of guidance, there's a good chance your child will look for someone new to emulate.

Q I have an older child my younger one wants to emulate, but the older one wants nothing to do with helping the younger one. How should I handle it?

A A great experience for an older sibling is to make time to support the development of a younger brother or sister. Being a younger sibling myself, I remember the excitement of having an older brother offer me advice, support, and direction in school and sports.

To entice an older brother or sister to take interest in helping a younger sibling, try praise. Compliment the older sibling's good qualities—such as leadership—or other qualities you would like passed on to a sister or brother.

Find a project where the older child can demonstrate a skill;
perhaps even reward him for doing a good job. The
opportunity to be responsible and to lead by example can
provide an older sibling with a great sense of self-awareness,
growth in communication skills, maturity, and self-
confidence. Brothers and sisters working together can also
strengthen the sibling bond with values of respect, trust,
and commitment to working as a team, all of which are
valuable for school, sport, and any career path.

When I was about 12 years old, I was participating in the long
jump in one of my first Junior Olympic Championships. At the
time of my competition, all of the coaches had other duties, so
my older brother Chris—who had long jump experience—
agreed to coach me. He helped me accurately measure out
my steps on the runway to make sure I hit the board with my
takeoff foot. I had competed well enough to be in the top three,
but I wasn't happy with second or third place; I competed to win.

I remember getting down to my last two attempts, and as
a result of not executing what my brother was telling me, or
what I knew to be efficient running and jumping technique, I
fouled my fifth jump and was left with one last attempt. My
brother told me to move my step back one foot. I thought he
was telling me to move it back so that I would end at least
with a fair jump and not foul on my last attempt. Fortunately,
he knew better than I that my competitiveness and passion to
win on my last attempt would push me to run faster down the
runway than I had on my warmup.

Sure enough, I flew down the runway. Even after moving my
step back a whole foot, I hit the board solidly and shot into the air
like a cannon. It felt awesome! When I landed in the sand, I
knew that I had jumped farther than all of my previous attempts.
But it wasn't until I heard the official announce the distance that I
knew I had jumped far enough to win the competition.

Older siblings have an opportunity to use their experiences and knowledge to support and teach a younger sibling, helping him to avoid the pitfalls they have already faced. My brother coached me to my one and only long jump Junior Olympic gold medal, and I clearly remember my parents being extremely proud of our collaborative effort.

Q My younger child tries to compete with her older sibling(s). How do I encourage her to not compare herself?

A It's a natural and healthy process for siblings to compare and compete with one another. There's no need to stop an instinctive behavior and potentially minimize your child's natural process of development. I also want you to consider what we've learned from research about older and younger children and their performance in sport—research that may help you guide your child.

When I was completing my doctorate in counseling psychology, I was able to collect data from 140 competitive Division 1 college track athletes, investigating the Effects of Sport Context and Birth Order on State Anxiety (2000). Findings demonstrated that firstborn athletes experienced significantly higher mental and emotional anxiety prior to performance than later-born athletes. In other research, Schachter (1959) suggested that firstborns experience higher levels of anxiety because parents have less patience with their firstborn children and offer more training with later-born children, which allows them to have lower levels of anxiety in high-anxiety situations. Further, Ideka and Myiashita (1983) proposed that firstborns are more likely to be pushed into sport competition and, as a result, perceive greater responsibility than later-borns to perform leadership duties.

Considering what we've learned from research, older siblings are likely to exhibit more anxiety as they forge their own path to live up to perceived expectations that they must be leaders, set an example, and perform well. As a parent, you want to support your older child's management of anxiety by helping her identify her particular anxiety sources and develop successful response tools, such as thought stopping, positive self-talk, and effective breathing (see appendices A–F). In addition, encourage your younger child to watch and learn from an older sibling's experience.

Q My child is beginning to adopt bad habits of other children in the sport to fit in. How do I deal with this?

A Remind your child why he is involved in sport and the positive attributes it offers. Refocus your child on the positive qualities you want him to develop, such as respect, integrity, or courage. Also restate your family rules and how you expect your child to behave.

Similarly, reiterate the rules and expectations of participating in the sport. Remind yourself and your child that playing a sport is a privilege, similar to getting a treat, going to a birthday party, or having computer time. Privileges should be taken away when your child exhibits poor behavior and rules are broken. There are positive and fun ways to fit in without developing bad habits and demonstrating poor behavior—reinforce the behavior you want your child to develop, focusing on the desired positive routines instead of the unwanted bad habits.

One great tool I've used is to introduce the "Word of the Week," which is written and posted somewhere visible, with a definition and example of how the word can be used. Discuss the word and use it as often as possible during conversation, and relate it to performance to reinforce understanding and application. This word game can strengthen your child's vocabulary, as well as reinforce the behavior you want to see on the playing field.

For example, if you use the word "courage," provide a definition. Then ask your child to use "courage" in a sentence that applies to sport, such as: "It takes courage to do the right thing at practice when my teammates aren't doing the right thing." Encourage your child to be courageous during practices and competition by taking responsibility for his personal behavior and focusing on how he can do better. By putting good examples in front of your child, he will build personal strengths and likely energize teammates to follow in his footsteps.

Q My child's coach is a terrible role model. Is that reason to take my child off the team? If so, how should I explain it to my child? Should I be honest with the coach?

A If you believe your child is receiving mixed or inappropriate messages, it is your duty to protect and provide the positive images and messages that your child receives. Young children look up to and seek the approval of coaches, who are given the responsibility to be authority figures.

If the coach is a poor role model, absolutely take the appropriate steps to protect your child from unnecessary harm. If you know in advance that a coach will not provide the example or model you believe to be appropriate for your child, you can ask the league or organization to switch your child to another team before the first practice. If you become aware of the coach's poor example during the season, find another team or league that your child can transfer to and then remove your child from the current team.

You can explain to the coach that your child will no longer participate with the team because another opportunity became available to play for a great coach who will provide terrific instruction and set a positive example for your child. Explain to your child the benefits of consistent positive messages that reinforce your family values, and your responsibility to place positive examples in her life, which you will seek out in her next coach. If the training and competition days for the new team are different, you can also explain that the new schedule was a better fit for your family.

Also consider writing a letter to league officials, explaining why you have decided to remove your child. Other parents may have expressed similar concerns, and with documentation the league can hopefully make a decision about removing the coach for the best interest of the children and program.

While your child is young, you will make the decision about who will coach her; however, you can give her the foundation now that will allow her to make that decision in the future. As our children grow older and continue their sport careers at various levels, the chance of encountering different types of coaches increases. You or your child may experience a coach who is difficult to get along with or has different approaches to teaching, mentoring, or life. As a parent, provide a solid foundation of values and morals that you and your family believe are necessary, and carry them through sport. As your child has the opportunity to learn from various coaches, she can evaluate how the coach delivers teachable moments based on the foundation of strong morals and values established in your family. If or when there are contradictions or outright offenses to that foundation, your child will have the knowledge and opportunity to decide what is in her best interest.

❖   ❖   ❖

Q   My child is the best on the team, and his teammates have begun to shun him out of jealousy. Now my child doesn't want to do as well. What do I do?

A   In my experience, people tend to gravitate toward someone who performs well to learn what makes him perform at a higher level, and how to duplicate his success. But with children or those who are less mature, jealousy and subsequent distancing can occur to avoid an undesirable comparison to someone with greater talent.

For instance, a child may make fun of or tease another kid for thinking he's special because he gets to play the whole game and score most of the points, accusing the child of being a ball hog. The accuser highlights the success of the teammate in a negative way, hoping to encourage him to change.

In this example, it sounds as if the accuser wants the accused to share the ball to allow other players opportunities to score or get more playing time. To manage the situation, the accused may consider sharing scoring opportunities or offering to sit out portions of a game to allow other kids more time to play. Another approach may be to bring the concern to the coach, who with greater awareness can support each player's performance opportunities. However, when pressure rises and performance suffers, the better players will most likely be asked to play. Part of being a good or great athlete is knowing how to manage critics, while still performing at your highest level.

If this situation arises with your child, take the opportunity to teach him that those who shun him because of his greatness are distancing themselves from their own opportunity for greatness, then encourage him to share some of his standout techniques with others, if it is appropriate, to help him hone his leadership skills.

When it comes to role models, my father was one of the best. He had three golden rules as a coach, and over the years—as a player, coach, and sport psychologist—I have found them to be invaluable. I hope you will too.

COACH FLOWERS' GOLDEN RULE #1

Maintaining a basic level of fitness and endurance is crucial to your athletic progress.

My father predicted that having the endurance, power, and speed to run a fast quarter mile would provide the base needed to achieve success in a variety of athletic endeavors, not just track. Using that golden rule time and time again, he was able to find or develop talent that may never have surfaced in some athletes. His insight into speed and endurance training was accompanied by his astute awareness of the body's need for water, especially during physical activity.

COACH FLOWERS' GOLDEN RULE #2

Water is a necessity.

My father encouraged the consumption of 8–10 glasses of water a day to keep the body hydrated and muscles loose and free of cramping and tearing, and he used the time devoted to water breaks to provide more instruction or to get feedback from the athletes he trained. On his watch, every minute was a chance to instruct!

FACTS ABOUT WATER

Are you drinking enough water? We all know that water is important, but you may be surprised (even shocked!) at how much is actually needed. Here are some enlightening statistics:

* 75% percent of Americans are chronically dehydrated.
* In 37% of Americans, the thirst mechanism is so weak that it is often mistaken for hunger.
* Even mild dehydration will slow down one's metabolism as much as 3%.
* One glass of water shuts down midnight hunger pangs for almost 100% of the dieters followed in a University of Washington study.
* Lack of water is the #1 trigger of daytime fatigue.

- Preliminary research indicates that 8–10 glasses of water a day could significantly ease back and joint pain for up to 80% of sufferers.

- A mere 2% drop in body water can trigger fuzzy short-term memory, trouble with basic math, and difficulty focusing on the computer screen.

- Drinking 5 glasses of water daily decreases the risk of colon cancer by 45%.

- Water can slash the risk of breast cancer by 79%, and those who drink one glass of water daily are 50% less likely to develop bladder cancer.

Are you drinking the amount of water
you should every day?

Coach Flowers' Golden Rule #3

All aches and pains should be iced.

My dad wasn't talking about a major injury, but the "hurt" that happens when you reach an untapped area of muscle rigor mortis, or fall during rough play. Most hurts can be cured with 20 minutes of icing the bothersome area. And if 20 minutes is not enough, repeat the process three to five times a day until the pain goes away. In fact, he believed in it so much, he often said, "Ice it, you'll feel better!" when it had nothing to do with a body part. His athletes eventually learned he was really talking about attitude.

My dad had enough insight to know that most young athletes weren't necessarily experiencing a physical hurt when they "limped" off the playing field. In many cases, he recognized that emotional or mental hurt was causing the pain, and that icing for a few minutes provided an athlete the opportunity to rest, recuperate, and refocus—and it gave my dad a chance to think of the "real" solution to an athlete's dilemma.

Injuries, like a pulled muscle or broken bone, are something entirely different. They require more attention, and

Coach Flowers was a steadfast believer that if you are injured, you need to see a doctor immediately. Fathers, mothers, family members, and coaches are not qualified to treat and diagnose. As a former athlete himself, my dad knew that loved ones and coaches do not always give the best advice—and many times provide inaccurate health information.

Most coaches today would probably consider my dad "old school." Nevertheless, he was a great youth coach who helped produce some of the greatest athletic talent in the state of Washington. He did so with ice, water, and a quarter mile of training.

7

CAR
and
HOME TALK

What to Discuss
and When

As a child, I thought my father was the master of the car-ride conversation. He could fill any jaunt with an unbelievable amount of information about a variety of topics, encouraging us to learn and participate in the dialogue. While my brother and I would sometimes wish we could just ride in silence, I now appreciate how much time he spent talking to us. Nowadays, kids are often in the back seat, preoccupied with some electronic gadget such that conversation with parents is all but lost.

There is no technology that can replace conversation with your child, no matter the age or topic. This chapter is therefore focused on how and when to have the most productive conversation with your young athlete to help her be appropriately encouraged, focused, and inspired in her sport(s), without losing sight of what else is important.

Q Should we discuss a performance during the drive home?

A Why not? Discussing performance can be enjoyable, memorable, and entertaining for the whole family. Feedback about your child's performance can be encouraged when it comes from a supportive place. Discuss the highlights and memorable moments to engrain positive memories; however, remember that your child just spent time at practice or competition with a coach and teammates who provided him with feedback, and the best feedback is in the moment. Because of that, don't be surprised or hurt if your young athlete is no longer interested in talking about his performance, especially if the feedback is critical, negative, or confrontational—this type should definitely be avoided.

Remember your audience is a young child who is building basic skills and learning how to compete. Unlike the overzealous parent, he is likely not concerned with being the best, not yet. Critiquing and harping about what mistakes were made and what could have been better will create a negative imprint in your child's mind about performing, especially in front of a parent.

Growing up in Seattle, my family lived in a house that was surrounded by hills. Every trip out of the neighborhood took us up and down a hilly street called Graham—a street my brother and I dreaded because my dad would use that 30 seconds to two minutes to lecture, depending on the weather. Hard rain, black ice, and snow would make Graham hill a tough road to drive, which could shut down conversation. But when the weather was good, no topic was off limits. We heard about school, communication, sports, fashion, relationships, family life, bathroom etiquette, and cooking, to name just a few of our dad's life lessons. Hunkered down in the back seat, we gave Graham Street a name that was our secret: "Lecture Hill."

This street was where my brother and I were told what we should focus on to perform well going into practice and competition; on the way home, we heard closing arguments for how we could improve during our next opportunity to practice or compete. As we aged, my brother and I found opportunities to turn what we felt were lectures into informational discussions and learning moments. But as kids, I remember feeling that those talks were major distractions to thinking about the cartoon I watched before leaving the house, what I did with my Evel Knievel action figure, who I was looking forward to seeing at practice/competition, or what I was going to eat when I finally got home. That was back in the day when young kids didn't have movies playing in the car, tablets, handheld computers, and mp3 players streaming live music—and they had attention spans longer than a blip!

Yes, use your time in the car to and from your child's practices and competitions to talk about sport in a healthy way. Ask about your child's experiences, and encourage positive play and teachable moments. Discuss the fun and memorable parts, but remember: the best time and place to teach your child about sport performance is in the moments when they occur.

❖   ❖   ❖

Q   Is mealtime a good time to discuss a performance?

A   Similar to a drive home after performance, mealtime is a stationary time when you can have your child's undivided attention to talk about sport. Again, it should be an enjoyable conversation that touches on the highlights of performance and provides an opportunity for your child to express her thoughts and feelings. If your objective is to teach your child something about her performance at mealtime, remember that young children will learn more during interactive and engaging play activities than they will learn through conversation.

Parents should be aware of how long they talk, and they should stop when the conversation becomes a monologue or lecture. Talk *with* your child, not at your child. Engage her in a two-way conversation with open-ended questions to evoke open and honest dialogue. If you find your conversation becoming one-sided where you are doing all of the talking, or you are asking complicated questions, your child may feel backed into a corner, looking for responses to please you.

Look for the following cues as a parent to let you know you may have gotten off track with your approach or tone:

❖ Your child is pushing food around the plate or not eating.

❖ She is not making eye contact.

❖ She is repeating words you have used in an effort to please you.

❖ She is giving short, yes/no answers, trying to change the subject, complaining, or even crying.

❖ Your child definitely wants to call it quits when she finally leaves the table.

Remember: Meals should be associated with favorable family time, not an anticipated period of criticism or unpleasantness.

Q   My spouse won't stop talking about the practice or competition. I know he/she means well, but it's affecting our family in a negative way. What do I do?

A   Away from your children, talk to your spouse about what you are seeing and experiencing, and help your spouse understand the impact his/her behavior is having on the family. If the situation becomes extreme, you may want to record or video the behavior and show it to your spouse. Be ready to offer suggestions that can positively change the family dynamics.

For example, offer your spouse a window of five minutes to ask open-ended questions about practice or competition. Encourage him/her to use an "inside voice" (or what some call a "library voice") when talking to your child about sport. Also, persuade your spouse to use his/her own personal outlet—such as exercise, reading, or gardening—to release the emotion, energy, or pressure he/she has as a result of watching a child perform. Lastly, reward your spouse when he/she gives positive feedback about your child's performance.

This could be an example of a parent who is living vicariously through his/her child, and in turn placing unfair pressure and expectation on the child to perform. Suggest to the spouse that he/she may release pent-up energy and the urge to perform by taking up his/her own sport or extracurricular activity.

Q

What are the best things to focus on when discussing a performance?

A

It's always best to first remember that a young child's performance will not be perfect; there will always be room for improvement, as it should be. A conversation about what could be done better could last a very long time, much longer than your child's attention to or interest in the subject. The better approach is to find as many positive things about a child's performance as you can, and discuss those with the intent of building and reinforcing his confidence and personal performance. Take note of what your child has accomplished, such as:

- ❖ areas of performance that have improved
- ❖ showing positive emotions during performance
- ❖ demonstrating good sportsmanship
- ❖ listening to the coach
- ❖ following rules
- ❖ trying new opportunities

Keep in mind that when you talk about a game or performance, maintain your child's level of understanding and appreciation. Your child is not competing for an Olympic medal; discussing strategy, player match-ups, or team and player statistics will likely cause your child to lose interest. Instead, engage him with simple things he can understand, such as how to move his body during play, what to look at or listen to while playing, who to play with, and the boundaries of the field of play. Above all, focus yours and your child's attention on how he can have fun, be healthy, and learn through play.

Q   How much should I allow my child to "vent" after a performance she wasn't happy about?

A   After a poor performance, it can be beneficial to give in to feelings of disappointment, sadness, frustration, and anger; holding on to or putting off these emotions can create an unpredictable explosion of emotion.

Particularly with children, you want to teach them how to acknowledge and appropriately release emotion. A 20- to 30-minute window for venting after an unwanted performance can be a healthy way to release the emotional burden and move on. Be available to your child to help her know that it is appropriate to feel frustrated, angry, sad, or disappointed, and offer methods to release and manage emotions, such as:

- talking with you openly
- telling a story about what she is feeling
- drawing a picture of what she is feeling
- simply being loved by you

At a young age, some children may not have the vocabulary to describe what they feel, so body language and behavior may be the predictors of feelings. Be aware of significant changes in body language, like sunken shoulders, low head, or heavy eyes and mouth, and look for a significant change in behavior, such as a lack of interest in food or playful activities, more aggressive behavior, or avoidance. Allow your child time to release emotions, recompose herself, and reconnect to the team, family, or friends.

Q Should I as a parent put a limit on the time we
   spend discussing the sport?

A There is no denying that sports have become a major part
   of and serve a vital role in our American lifestyle—you can
   turn on your television at any hour and find a show about
   sports. However, as a parent, you want to raise a well-
   rounded child, so it's important to talk about the other
   things going on in your child's life, such as school,
   scouting, music, and other extracurricular activities and
   interests. Religion and spirituality are also valuable
   discussion topics you may embrace in your family.

   Remember that children tend to get excited about
   birthdays, holidays, and vacations—these, too, can offer a
   break from sport. Toys, television, and video games may
   intervene, but my all-time favorite is getting kids off the
   couch and outside for some good old-fashioned,
   unorganized play.

Building Character

Values, Feedback & Rewards

"My attitude is that if you push me towards something that you think is a weakness, then I will turn that perceived weakness into a strength."

—MICHAEL JORDAN

Your experiences as a parent have likely helped you identify what are important values, beliefs, and skills you would like to share with your child. Her participation in sport can help build and solidify those that you teach at home; it can also encourage her to push beyond her boundaries of comfort to learn a new skill, see a game from a different perspective, develop social skills and team dynamics, or maintain the pleasure of playing. These same skills can be applied to the larger game of life.

Consider how you manage and present your own values, beliefs, or skills to your child as you help her build character through sport. Your child will embody your attitude and behaviors more than the words you say, so embrace a positive attitude as you teach your child sound fundamentals of sport through positive play.

Q What are the crucial elements of character building I should be focused on with my child at this age?

A This question commands a multifaceted answer, as there are several components that are vital.

First, an important characteristic of early athletic development is enjoyment. Athletic participation should be centered on enjoying the activities and opportunities offered through sport. When sport participation is fun, kids want to attend practice, learn new skills, and accept challenges to improve their performance. Having fun allows them to enjoy new social interactions, build friendships, and experiment with diverse social situations. With pleasure as the nucleus, additional personal characteristics can flourish, forming a solid foundation and becoming crucial elements of personal development in the areas of motivation, respect, discipline, self-awareness, responsibility, and self-confidence.

MOTIVATION

Your child needs to have a basic desire to participate in the sport, and it's important that the motivation to perform comes from the child, not the parent. Without motivation, it will be harder for your child to train, learn, grow, accept challenge, fail, and excel. Motivation is a fundamental skill needed for training and competition. Young children may occasionally need an outside source (coach, trainer, training partner, family, friends) to stimulate motivation, but the initial drive and passion to perform should reside inside your child.

As a parent, you can stimulate motivation by describing how much fun your child will have playing a sport. For example, explain how exciting it will be to:

❖ play with friends and to make new friends
❖ learn how to play the sport he watches on TV or that he plays in a video game
❖ get new athletic equipment

Taking your child to a local competition of the sport he is interested in playing can spark motivation; sometimes your child may need it to train or perform at a higher level. Setting training goals and using positive cues of reinforcement, such as "I will work hard every day to achieve my goal" can provide motivation to continue training and push through slumps.

RESPECT

In sport, children need to learn to respect the athletic environment, the same way they learn to take care of their toys or bedroom at home. Young athletes must learn to attend to their equipment and respect the code of conduct for an athletic venue.

For example, entering a basketball gym and walking directly onto the court during play or practice can get a child run over, hit by a ball, or provoke a strong reaction from the coach or players on the floor. In this case, your child would be taught to pay attention and to respect the rules of the court. Athletes may also be asked to put their bags, drinks, and personal belongings outside the performance area to respect the field of play.

As a parent, you play an important role in teaching your child to respect the coach. Explain to your child that the coach becomes the responsible adult when she is at practice or in competition. A good coach will explain team rules and expectations at the beginning of the season. These may include being respectful when a child talks to teammates or the coach. For example, a coach may require his athletes to respond to instructions by saying "yes, coach" to make sure they are listening and understand his directions. He may further request that athletes not talk when he is speaking to demonstrate respect for his authority. You can help your child adapt by talking about why honoring rules and showing respect will make her athletic experience more enjoyable.

DISCIPLINE AND SELF-AWARENESS

Following rules and instructions, being on time for practices and performances, completing all performances (great and not so great), and maintaining a healthy diet are a few examples of the things your child will need to learn to have a great sport experience, all of which will demand discipline.

To help your child, teach him the values of being on time for meals at home or cleaning up toys or activities. It may feel repetitive because it is. You will state and restate the same requests to emphasize the importance of being on time or cleaning a room, but teaching self-awareness and discipline also requires positive reinforcement of desired behaviors. Develop favorable responses to offer your child when he is on time for meals or cleans up his room. The positive changes you see in your child's self-awareness and discipline at home should also be seen in his sport performance.

As your child trains to develop new and improved performance skills, then uses those skills in competition against other athletes, you should see his self-awareness blossom. He will become more able to recognize a great performance (for his age group) versus not so good, difficulty performing a skill versus ease, and giving full effort versus hardly trying.

RESPONSIBILITY

With greater self-awareness and discipline, your child will likely develop better understanding of the commitment she must make to enjoy sport and to have a great performance. Areas where your child can take responsibility include:

- completing homework and chores before playing
- getting dressed in her uniform and having equipment ready before practices or competitions without a reminder
- working on improving skills, without much prodding
- knowing the rules and tenets of the sport

SELF-CONFIDENCE

Sport can be a great vehicle for helping your child gain confidence in his ability to perform and become a successful athlete. Managing fears about new experiences in sport, building new athletic skills, and sharpening existing talents provide great strength-based learning for your child, which promotes self-confidence. With confidence as a foundational strength, your child will find pleasure in sport performance, adapt a willingness to take risks and build new skills, and likely develop an increased motivation to continue in sport and other unfamiliar opportunities.

I once worked with a young South-American female tennis player who described herself as quick and athletic, with good court vision and solid racket skills. She was slight in stature and stood about 5'4". She was a successful singles player with confidence in her skills; yet, when she faced a taller, stronger opponent like Serena Williams, she became afraid, timid, and lost confidence.

The young South-American focused more on the stature and presence of her opponent than she did on her own talents and performance. She was swept away by the media hype, attention, and perceived threat of playing the #1 seeded player, and as a result, lost focus on her own performance strengths. She needed to regain, reframe, and refocus her attention on her own performance skills, the strengths she possessed, and how to successfully execute her strengths during performance. Believing in her strengths, focusing on how to use them, and taking ownership of her own performance allowed her to play with greater self-confidence.

Q How can I best help my child see the value of being a team player?

A If you watch young children play, you may notice that they play primarily to please themselves, not others. That's especially true if they have not yet learned to share or work with others. To get the idea across of what it means to be part of a team, don't just talk about it—demonstrate. Young children learn better through an activity.

For example, play a game (such as ping pong doubles), where players are divided into teams, to show your child what it's like to play within a team, support a teammate, share the ball, and communicate with others. You can also watch an athletic game on TV with your child and point out positive team performance. When you see a good example of a team working together, direct your child's attention to the positive emotions and actions that occur, such as players giving each other a high five or teammates cheering on the sideline. You want your child to make the emotional connection between feeling good and working together as a team.

Things you do every day as a family can also provide good examples of teamwork, such as preparing a meal together or helping siblings with chores.

Q   Should winning be important?

A   The reality is that our society puts a lot of emphasis on winning. At very early ages, children are taught that winning brings a lot of rewards—from a gold star for a job well done, to trophies for finishing in first place, to cash for a top performer. The challenge for parents is to create balance so that young athletes understand they reap benefits from simply playing a sport, win or lose. To that end, take the focus off winning and emphasize building strong skills, performing well, being part of a team effort, playing well with others, and enjoying the athletic experience.

It's sad and embarrassing to see adults become so consumed with their child's athletic success that their zeal affects the child's performance, as illustrated in the following example.

During a championship game, a parent of an eight year-old basketball player got so upset with a referee's calls that he began yelling at him. The child was embarrassed and distracted by his parent's behavior, which resulted in the athlete making mistakes and turning the ball over. The child's attention was on the parent and not the game; the parent became the point of focus. Because of the parent's poor behavior, he had to be removed from the gym before the game could continue. The child continued playing but appeared distracted the remainder of the game.

While basketball is a highly competitive sport where high school and college scouts are following talented players at a very early age, winning or losing a basketball game at eight years old will not determine a child's future. It may, however, determine the immediate future of an out-of-control parent, not to mention a strong negative message sent to your child about the importance of winning above all else.

Q What are appropriate rewards for playing/doing well? Should I be careful about offering material rewards for good performances?

A While many children and parents begin their participation in sports with hope of having a future high school experience, opportunities to become intercollegiate athletes, or even professional careers, the latter of these is unfortunately the least likely. Therefore, it's important to remember that the effort you put into feeding your child's *internal* desire to play will reap the best reward and be the greatest motivator.

PROGRESSION OF STUDENT-ATHLETES FROM HIGH SCHOOL
TO NCAA TO PROFESSIONAL SPORTS

STUDENT ATHLETES	MEN'S BASKETBALL	WOMEN'S BASKETBALL	FOOTBALL	BASEBALL	MEN'S ICE HOCKEY	MEN'S SOCCER
High School	538,676	433,120	1,086,627	474,791	35,198	410,982
High School Seniors	153,907	123,749	310,465	135,655	10,057	117,423
NCAA	17,984	16,186	70,147	32,450	3,964	23,365
NCAA Freshman Roster Positions	5,138	4,.625	20,042	9,271	1,133	6,676
NCAA Seniors	3,996	3,597	15,588	7,211	881	5,192
NCAA Drafted	46	32	254	678	7	101
% High School to NCAA	3.3%	3.7%	6.5%	6.8%	11.3%	5.7%
% NCAA to Pro	1.2%	0.9%	1.6%	9.4%	0.8%	1.9%
% High School to Pro	0.03%	0.03%	0.08%	0.50%	0.07%	0.09%

courtesy www.ncaa.org

Rewards of athletic competition can definitely contribute to why and how athletes compete—at any age. Self-gratification, the psychological boost of being acknowledged, the praise or applause from family, friends, and fans, and the tangible trophy are all fantastic, but even more so is competing for the personal gratification of identifying a desired goal, building a path for accomplishment, and achieving the desired outcome through successful perform-ance. Such an athlete finds reward in personal improvement and will likely concentrate less on the material or superficial reward opportunities, marking the difference between extrinsically and intrinsically motivated athletes.

At this young age, you'll definitely want to emphasize building intrinsic rewards within your child, as this foundation will be crucial for sport participation—and life in general. For this reason, I will go into a bit more detail on how to achieve this as a parent.

Intrinsic sources of motivation are interests or desires that encourage you to pursue a desired outcome. For example, my desire to improve my foot speed simply to become a faster runner is an intrinsic source of motivation. I'm working toward a goal I've set for myself, and I'll be the one to determine my level of satisfaction, which is the ultimate reward. Because they're within our control, intrinsic sources of motivation can be created, managed, and achieved by the individual without outside interference or influence.

Extrinsic sources of motivation, on the other hand, are influences or desires that are outside of our control, such as trophies, hugs, high fives, money, or endorsements. The trouble with extrinsic motivation is that if those factors aren't available to an athlete, where will he find the motivation to reach his goals? The reaction from others and the tangible things being offered for successful perform-ances are highly desirable, but since they are not always available, extrinsic motivation will likely fluctuate and possibly be lost.

The counter to seeking or providing the external reward is identifying the internal source of motivation for your child. By doing so, you are clarifying his personal desires and what is truly going to make performing a happy and successful experience. With this identified source of pleasure, your child will have the desire, initiative, determination, and commitment to pursue and make sacrifices to attain a goal. As your child continues to compete and enjoy sport, he will experience the personal gratification of achieving:

- ❖ what he set out to accomplish
- ❖ the success of making progress in his physical, mental, emotional, and spiritual abilities
- ❖ the success of learning from past mistakes
- ❖ the success from making improvements in who he is as a human being

Internal motivation is an undeniable source of motivation that cannot be taken away. You therefore want to teach your child that he and only he has the power to control or alter it.

Below are examples of intrinsic and extrinsic sources of motivation. Identify those that apply to your child.

INTRINSIC MOTIVATORS

- ❖ The child's purpose for the activity
- ❖ What he wants from participation
- ❖ His identified strengths
- ❖ His identified areas of development
- ❖ What he will work toward improving

EXTRINSIC MOTIVATORS

- Awards
- Treats
- Recognition
- Acceptance
- Friendships

The following are sources of internal motivation that can be used as the foundation for athletic involvement and encourage the desire to pursue athletic success:

- GOAL ACHIEVEMENT
  (e.g., successfully completing training or conditioning camps, completing the season without complaining)

- CULTURAL PRIDE
  (e.g., commitment to personal identity development and respect for team values)

- INTERNAL DESIRE
  (e.g., using enjoyment of sport to improve self-awareness and personal growth)

- TASK DEVELOPMENT
  (e.g., building body awareness, self-esteem, agility, balance, coordination, and sport-specific skills)

- PROCESS DEVELOPMENT
  (e.g., being a team player, developing and following a plan/routine for practice/competition, and building athletic skills)

Q   What are some ways I can encourage internal
     rewards for my child?

A   Finding the appropriate combination of internal motivation
     and reward is critical to successful performance. Below are
     tactics to increase your chance of helping your child
     develop a positive frame of mind toward athletics.

     ❖ "GUARANTEE" SUCCESS
        Structure your child's activities, both individually and
        as part of a team, in ways that ensure success by using
        effort or improvement as goals rather than performance
        outcomes or winning. Give repeated opportunities to
        perform successful skills during practice.

     ❖ GIVE YOUR CHILD A ROLE IN GOAL SETTING
        AND DECISION-MAKING
        Feelings of self-control directly improve intrinsic
        motivation. Input from your child, particularly as she
        gains more experience, can guide personal develop-
        ment. This is an excellent way to improve feelings of
        individual satisfaction.

     ❖ PRAISE PERFORMANCE, NOT PERSONALITY OR
        CHARACTER
        Address your child's behaviors, efforts, and accom-
        plishments that warrant praise, not his character or
        personality. Praising your child's actions with specific
        performance-based feedback offers tangible and
        concrete information about competence. This also
        enhances positive self-evaluation and reinforces social
        confidence.

❖ FACILITATE PERCEPTIONS OF COMPETENCE

Set realistic goals and use personal comparisons as reliable sources of competence. For example, acknowledge your child's ability and skill to control the ball while dribbling through cones on the first day of practice, then four weeks later. By acknowledging a significant improvement in skills and abilities, you can facilitate the development of your child's competence. Providing rewards may also improve intrinsic motivation, if the reward supports feelings of competence.

❖ USE VARIABLE RATHER THAN CONSTANT REINFORCEMENT

You can prolong the benefits of positive feedback using intermittent reinforcement, rather than constant. Variable reinforcement allows time for the effects of learning, practice, and training to be demonstrated as improvement, which in turn will improve internal motivation. For example, offer reinforcement after reaching a set goal or demonstrating desirable performance.

❖ VARY CONTENT AND SEQUENCE OF PRACTICE DRILLS

Boredom is an enemy of athletic participation and intrinsic motivation because it is the antithesis of fun. Lack of enjoyment is a primary reason for dropping out of sport, so it's crucial to make practice pleasant and exciting by:

    ❖ filling it with opportunities to learn

    ❖ demonstrating new skills

    ❖ engaging in simulated competition

❖   employing fun tasks such as obstacle courses or
    relay races

❖   playing different games for conditioning

In order for your child to maintain a desire for sport
participation, she may be strongly influenced by how she
thinks about her performance and the experience of the
activity. Creating a positive approach to athletics is
therefore vital if you want to override the not-so-fun
moments. Let's face it: children may not always be excited
to see the coaches, parents, or teammates around them.
During these times, thought stopping and positive
thinking will come in handy (see Appendix A and B for
more on these topics). In other words, the less time an
athlete spends worrying or feeling irritated, and the more
time spent developing strengths for a successful performance, the better off she'll be. Bottom line: By limiting
negative thinking and focusing on a positive approach to
improving performance, she'll increase her internal drive
and ability to perform.

❖   ❖   ❖

Q   **What types of feedback should I give my child?
    Which types should I avoid?**

A   Since children look to their parents to set an example, you
    are the role model for a number of things that will
    determine your child's behavior as an athlete, including
    responsibility, independence, motivation, discipline, and
    honesty. The feedback you provide can encourage your
    child's development of the necessary fundamentals, so it's

vital to recognize there are two types of feedback—
undesired and desired—and how the two are delivered.

UNDESIRED FEEDBACK

❖ Negative or deriding comments about what could
have been better

❖ No reaction at all

❖ Recognizing/applauding everyone or everything
except your child

❖ Ignoring your child's participation

❖ Not being present

DESIRED FEEDBACK

❖ Affirming statements, such as: "Congratulations!"
"You did a good job!" and "You looked like you
were having fun!"

❖ A pat on the back or hug

❖ Positive recognition of what was done well
(specific skill, play, interaction)

❖ Excitement in your voice (even if you don't know
how to articulate what was good about your
child's participation)

Clearly, keeping your focus on desired feedback will have a
positive effect on your child, which should always be your
goal as a parent. As such, be aware of moments where you
may lapse into undesired feedback, and rely on the desired
feedback examples above to get you back on track. Both
you and your child will reap the rewards!

CONCLUSION

If you have come this far in the book, you are clearly dedicated to being a great parent who is willing to support your child. I hope the questions, answers, and real-life examples offer some insight into how you can successfully introduce your child to sports, and reassure you that you have the tools to help your child have a satisfying and long-lasting athletic experience. Your interest, involvement, and commitment to providing a stable foundation for your child will pay dividends to your child's future in sport—and in life.

Enjoy the journey!

Appendix

Thought Stopping

WHAT IS THOUGHT STOPPING?

Thought stopping can help you overcome the nagging worry and doubt that stands in the way of relaxation by addressing intrusive, unrealistic, and unproductive thoughts that often lead to anxiety, self-doubt, and defeat, such as: "I can't do it," "I hate myself," "I'll never be able to achieve my goals," or "If I don't win first place, I'll die."

Thought stopping involves concentrating on the unwanted or irrational thoughts, then suddenly stopping and emptying your mind. The command "stop" or a loud noise is generally used to interrupt the unpleasant thoughts. Thought stopping is successful because:

(1) The command "stop" serves as an awakening to inhibit the negative behavior.

(2) The command "stop" acts as a distractor.

(3) "Stop" is an assertive response and can be followed by thought substitutions of positive self-talk or reassuring statements. It has been well documented that negative feelings and behavior consistently follow negative thoughts, so if the thoughts can be controlled, stress and anxiety levels can be managed.

SYMPTOM RELIEF

Using thought stopping can reduce thoughts of failure and grandeur, impulses leading to tension, and anxiety attacks.

TIME FOR MASTERY

Effective mastery can occur when thought stopping is practiced conscientiously throughout the day for three days to one week.

THOUGHT STOPPING EXERCISES

The following thought-stopping exercises can help your child reduce, if not stop, negative thoughts that stand in the way of positive performance. I have found these exercises particularly helpful with children who are anxious, seek perfection, and are easily frustrated by poor performance.

AIDED THOUGHT INTERRUPTION

(1) Close your eyes and imagine a situation in which a stressful thought is likely to occur or has occurred. Try to include normal as well as irrational and negative thinking. In this way, you can interpret the stressful thoughts while allowing a continuing flow of healthy thinking.

(2) Set a timer for three minutes.

(3) Look away from the timer, close your eyes, and think about your stressful thought. When you hear the timer, shout "STOP!" You can also raise your hand or snap your fingers.

(4) Let your mind empty all of the negative and bothersome thoughts, leaving only the neutral and healthy thoughts.

(5) Try to keep neutral and healthy thoughts in mind for about 30 seconds after the "stop." If the upsetting thought returns during the 30 seconds, shout "STOP!" again.

UNAIDED THOUGHT INTERRUPTION

Take control of the thought-stopping cue without the use of a timer.

(1) Imagine a situation in which a stressful thought is likely to occur or has occurred. While contemplating the unwanted thought, shout "STOP!"

(2) When you have succeeded in extinguishing the thought on several occasions by shouting "STOP!", begin interrupting the thought with "stop" in a normal voice.

(3) Once you are able to stop the thought by using your normal voice, start interrupting the thought with "stop" in a whisper.

(4) When you are able to interrupt the anxiety-provoking thought with a whisper, use a non-verbal command of "stop." Imagine hearing "STOP!" shouted in your mind. Success at this level indicates that you can stop unwanted thoughts in public without calling attention to yourself.

Appendix

Positive Thinking and Positive Self-Talk

WHAT IS POSITIVE THINKING & POSITIVE SELF-TALK?

Positive thinking and self-talk consist of keeping thoughts in the affirmative to reinforce favorable ideas about yourself, which supports positive feelings and behaviors. You have the power to control what you think, feel, and do. To be positive, you must first think positive. The phrase, "I am happy" is a great use of positive thinking and self-talk to start your morning. Reinforce this positive self-talk with thoughts of what make you happy, such as:

- ❖ *I woke up in a bed this morning.*
- ❖ *I have a family who loves me.*
- ❖ *I am excited to play my sport.*

This routine will elicit positive emotions, and more often than not, be followed by positive behaviors.

Thought Substitution

In place of the unwanted, irrational, negative thoughts, create some positive or reassuring, assertive statements that would be appropriate for given situations. For example, if your child gets frustrated when trying to learn something new, teach her to say something to herself like: "This is challenging, but I can learn it by slowing down and taking it one step at a time." Develop several alternative statements your child can say to herself, since the same response may lose its power of significance through repetition.

Symptom Relief

Using positive thinking and positive self-talk can reduce anxiety, depression, rage, frustration, guilt, and a sense of worthlessness.

Positive Thinking & Positive Self-talk Exercise

Help your child create positive thinking and self-talk phrases to promote favorable feelings, beliefs, and desirable behaviors. Below are some examples of self-encouragement, self-control, and self-confidence to consider. Try these, then create your own positive thinking and self-talk words or phrases.

Self-Encouragement

Examples of self-encouragement phrases:

* ❖ "I'm doing great!"
* ❖ "Keep going!"
* ❖ "Stay on task."
* ❖ "Good job!"
* ❖ "I am the greatest!" (Mohammed Ali, the famous boxing champion, used this statement often. It is an example of displaying external confidence to build internal confidence.)

5 SELF-ENCOURAGEMENT WORDS/PHRASES I OR MY CHILD CAN USE

1.

2.

3.

4.

5.

SELF-CONTROL

Examples of phrases to generate self-control:

❖ "Concentrate on being smooth."

❖ "You're prepared, now execute your strategy."

❖ "Focus on yourself."

5 SELF-CONTROL WORDS/PHRASES I OR MY CHILD CAN USE

1.

2.

3.

4.

5.

SELF-CONFIDENCE

Examples of phrases to maintain self-confidence:

- ❖ "I can do this."
- ❖ "Focus on my strengths."
- ❖ "Focus on why I'm here."
- ❖ "Trust yourself and your training."

5 SELF-CONFIDENCE WORDS/PHRASES I OR MY CHILD CAN USE

1.

2.

3.

4.

5.

APPENDIX

Effective Breathing

WHAT IS EFFECTIVE BREATHING?

Abdominal or diaphragmatic breathing is the natural breathing pattern of newborn babies and sleeping adults, which is characterized by inhaling deeply into the lungs as the diaphragm contracts and exhaling as the diaphragm expands. Breathing is even and not constricted.

Muscle tension and anxiety that results from stressful situations and thoughts can be reduced by increasing your awareness of how you breathe and changing to more abdominal breathing, which can easily produce a state of relaxation, if done effectively.

SYMPTOM RELIEF

Using effective breathing exercises can help reduce irritability, muscle tension, headaches, fatigue, generalized anxiety disorders, panic attacks, agoraphobia, and depression. Breathing exercises can be used to treat and prevent hyperventilation, shallow breathing, and cold extremities.

TIME FOR MASTERY

Effective breathing patterns can be learned in just a few minutes and the benefits can be experienced immediately; however, the lasting effects of effective breathing exercises may not be fully appreciated until after months of application. Practice different breathing exercises and develop a breathing program that you and your child find most beneficial. Mastery will come with consistent practice.

BREATHING EXERCISES

The following effective breathing exercises can help your child manage and reduce anxiety and improve attention in the moment. These exercises can be practiced in different poses; however, it is recommended to lie on your back on something soft. Bend your knees and move your feet about shoulder width apart while ensuring that your spine is straight. Here is an effective deep breathing script you can read to your child.

EFFECTIVE DEEP BREATHING

1. Scan your body for tension.

2. Place one hand on your abdomen and one hand on your chest.

3. Inhale slowly and deeply through your nose into your abdomen to push up your hand as much as feels comfortable. Your chest should only move a little.

4. Exhale through your mouth, pushing a quiet and relaxing breath of air through your lips. Release all of the air in your lungs before taking in another breath. Your mouth, tongue, and jaw will be relaxed. Take long, slow, deep breaths that raise and lower your abdomen. Focus on the sound and feeling of breathing as you become more and more relaxed. Practice for a few seconds.

5. When you feel comfortable with abdominal breathing, practice it during the day, either sitting or standing. Focus on the air moving in and out of your lungs and your abdomen as it moves up and down. Feel the relaxation of deep breathing and practice it whenever you feel yourself getting tense.

Now let's practice another deep-breathing exercise. This one can also be used to release tension.

This exercise involves deep abdominal breathing with the addition of counting each time you exhale. As you take a deep breath in and slowly exhale, you will count "one" to yourself. Take another deep breath in and slowly exhale "two," and so on up to five.

You can count your exhalations in sets of five until you have reduced or released your feelings of tension. This is an abdominal breathing script you can read to your child.

1. Take a deep breath into your abdomen and hold it. Slowly exhale and say or think "one."
2. Take another deep breath in and hold it. Then slowly exhale, saying or thinking "two."
3. Again take a deep breath in and hold it. Slowly exhale while saying or thinking"three."
4. Continue breathing in, feeling relaxed and comfortable, and exhaling until you've reached five.
5. Now continue this style of breathing for another set of five.

Notice your breathing gradually slow down, feel your body relax, and experience your mind calming as you continue to practice this breathing exercise.

QUICK CALM

Now let's practice another deep-breathing exercise called a Quick Calm, which can be used in pressure situations or when you don't have much time to calm down. Quick Calm can be very effective prior to, during, or after a performance, competition, debate, argument, or stressful situation. Here is a quick calm script you can read to your child.

1. Take a deep breath into your abdomen, saying to yourself, "I'm calm."

2. Hold it. Then exhale saying, "I'm relaxed."

3. Continue this pattern of deep breathing, noticing your breathing gradually slowing down, feeling your body relax, and your mind calming.

4. Continue to practice this breathing exercise for the next 30 seconds.

Appendix

Progressive Relaxation

WHAT IS PROGRESSIVE RELAXATION?

Psychological stress wreaks havoc with the feeling of well-being in your body, which responds to anxiety-provoking thoughts and events with muscle tension. Progressive relaxation of your muscles reduces the tension in your body; it can also bring down your pulse rate, blood pressure, and perspiration and respiration rates. When deep muscle relaxation is successfully mastered, it can be used like an anti-anxiety pill.

Physiological or muscle tension increases your experience of anxiety, whereas deep muscle relaxation reduces physiological or muscle tension and is incompatible with anxiety.

Most people don't realize which of their muscles are chronically tense. Progressive relaxation provides a way of identifying particular muscles and muscle groups and distinguishing between sensations of tension and deep relaxation.

SYMPTOM RELIEF

It has been shown that progressive muscle relaxation can reduce muscular tension, anxiety, fatigue, muscle spasms, neck and back pain, stuttering, insomnia, depression, mild phobias, and high blood pressure.

TIME FOR MASTERY

With two 15-minute sessions per day, you can master progressive relaxation in one to two weeks.

PROGRESSIVE RELAXATION EXERCISES

The following progressive muscle relaxation exercises can help your child reduce physiological or muscle tension and become more aware of feeling relaxed muscles versus tense muscles, in order to improve performance. The exercise can be abbreviated to specific areas of the body in order to adjust the time requirement to your child's attention span.

SPECIAL CONSIDERATIONS

When you release the tension in a particular muscle, let it go instantly. A slower release of tension holds tension in the muscle.

BASIC PROCEDURE

Below is a progressive muscle relaxation exercise I use with young athletes to help them identify areas of the body and distinguish between a relaxed and a tense muscle.

Begin by finding a comfortable and quiet setting where you will not be disturbed. Have the child lie down on his/her back with arms and legs stretched out flat, breathing without any constrictions. Loosen any clothing that may restrict breathing or comfort. Then read the following script:

Close your eyes and take a deep breath in. Hold that breath for a count of 1 ... 2 ... and slowly exhale. Again, repeat the deep breath in, hold it for 1 ... 2 ... and slowly exhale. Continue with your deep breathing to gradually slow your heart rate and increase your focus on calm, easy breathing. With every breath you feel more calm and more relaxed. With this feeling of composure and relaxation, allow your body to release all tension, worry, and muscle pressure. Free your mind and body from every restriction. Allow yourself to feel relaxed and allow your body to freely exist. Continue breathing at a normal pace for yourself.

As I count down from 5 to 1, you will find yourself becoming more and more relaxed. You're in control of the process and you control how relaxed you want to get. In your mind, think of a place that is comfortable. 5 ... you're relaxed and you're comfortable ... 4 ... you're feeling calm and composed ... 3 ... allow yourself to freely float within your feeling of peace ... 2 ... you're at peace ... 1.

With your wonderful feelings of comfort and peace, let's begin to relax your muscles. For each of the following exercises, I want you to hold the pressure in your muscles for no more than five seconds and instantly release the muscle pressure.

Let's begin by raising your eyebrows as if you're trying to touch your hairline. Hold your eyebrows up ... hold them, hold them ... and lower them to a normal comfortable level. Feel the difference between tension and comfort. Again, raise your eyebrows to your hairline, hold it ... and release the tension to feel the warmth of a relaxed brow.

Now, keeping your eyes closed, put a frown on your face by pushing your eyebrows and eyes to the middle of your face. Press your lips together, and press your tongue against the roof of your mouth. Feel all of the pressure you have put into the middle of your face ... and relax, feeling the warmth of your blood flow through your face. Take a deep breath and relax with this warm sensation of blood flowing through your face.

Press your head as far back as you can go without injury. Try to put your head between your shoulder blades and experience the tension in your neck. Hold on ... and bring your head forward, allowing your head to go back to a comfortable, relaxed position. Now, bring your head forward and press your chin against your chest. Feel the tension in your throat and in the back of your neck. Hold that tension for a count of 1, 2, 3, 4, and 5. Now, move your head back to a resting position and relax.

Now, raise your shoulders as if you're trying to put them into your ears. Feel the pressure build and build ... and slowly release the pressure in your shoulders and neck and feel the flow of relaxation. Take in a deep breath and slowly exhale. Enjoy this feeling of relaxation. Experience the tingling of warm blood flowing through your neck and shoulders. If you need to shake out or rotate your shoulders or head to feel greater relaxation, please do so. Get accustomed to the warm feeling of blood flowing through your relaxed muscles. Allow the feeling of relaxation to get deeper and deeper.

Now, bend both of your elbows and tense your biceps. Tense them as hard as you can and observe the tightness. Feel the concentration of blood in the belly of your muscle. Hold it ... and slowly relax and straighten out your arms. Let the blood gradually flow through the rest of your arm so you can feel the warmth of relaxation pass through your arms. This is the desirable feeling of being relaxed.

Now, let's move to your hands. Clench both of your fists, tighter and tighter, studying the tension in your hands, wrists, and forearms. Hold it ... and reduce the pressure in your hands and fingers to feel the tingling and looseness in your hands. Notice the soothing feeling that now embodies your hands, fingers, wrists, and forearms. Again, clench your fists, noticing the tension and pressure. Hold it ... and relax to feel the pleasure of relaxation.

Now, allow your entire torso to relax. Experience the comfort and warmth of being relaxed. Take in a deep breath, completely filling your lungs. Hold it ... notice the tension ... and slowly exhale, allowing your breath to escape freely along with the tension in your body. Relax, letting your breath come freely and gently. Repeat this process, allowing the tension to escape from your body as you exhale every deep breath.

Next, tighten your stomach muscles and hold them. Feel the tension in your stomach and lower back ... hold it for a few seconds, and relax. Now place your hand on your stomach and take a deep breath in, allowing your abdomen to push your stomach and hand out. Exhale by pushing out your breath, allowing your hand to lower. Feel the pleasure of relaxation as the air rushes out and your body sinks deeper into its position of comfort.

Now, tighten your buttocks. Hold the pressure in the muscles ... and release the pressure and tension. Relax and feel the difference. Tighten your thighs by pressing your heels down as hard as you can. Now release the pressure. Relax and feel the pleasure of warm thigh muscles. Now, point your toes forward and flex your calves as tight as you can ... and relax. Now pull your toes back toward your head, tightening your shins. Pull it tight ... and relax. Feel the enjoyable difference in your warm, loose muscles.

Feel the warmth and heaviness throughout your lower body as the relaxation deepens. Relax your feet, ankles, calves, shins, knees, thighs, and buttocks. Let the relaxation spread to your stomach, lower back, and chest. Let yourself go and enjoy the warmth of being relaxed. Feel the warmth in your shoulders, arms, and hands. Notice the looseness and relaxation in your neck, jaw, and all of your facial muscles. Allow your body to completely relax. Enjoy the experience of a loose, relaxed mind and body.

BREATHING AND SHORTHAND PROGRESSIVE RELAXATION

Repeat each procedure at least once, tensing each muscle group for 5–7 seconds and then relaxing for 15–30 seconds. Notice the contrast between the sensations of tension and relaxation.

(1) Take a deep breath through your abdomen. Hold it 3–4 seconds, then exhale. Repeat 5–7 times.

(2) Curl both fists, tightening biceps and forearms. Hold, then relax.

(3) Pull up your eyebrows, trying to touch your hairline. Wrinkle your forehead and at the same time press your head as far back as possible and roll it to the right, making a complete circle. Then reverse directions. Now close your eyes, put a frown on your face by pushing your eyebrows and eyes to the middle of your face. Press your lips together, press your tongue against the roof of your mouth, and hunch your shoulders. Hold it, then relax.

(4) Pull your feet and toes back toward your head, tightening your shins. Hold it, then relax. Point your toes, tightening your calves, and simultaneously tighten your buttocks and thighs. Hold it, then relax.

(5) Take a deep breath through your abdomen. Hold it 3–4 seconds, then exhale. Repeat 5–7 times.

APPENDIX

Visualization

WHAT IS EFFECTIVE VISUALIZATION?

You can significantly reduce stress with the power of your imagination. You also can increase the likelihood of successful performance with repeated and deliberate visualization of successful performance. The power of the imagination far exceeds that of the will. It's hard to will yourself into a relaxed state, but you can imagine relaxation spreading through your body, and you can visualize yourself performing successfully. Imagination can be used to help you learn how to draw on your body's healing power in times of stress, and during performance.

SYMPTOM RELIEF

Visualization is effective in treating many stress-related and physical illnesses, including headaches, muscle spasms, chronic pain, and general or situation-specific anxiety. Repeating deliberate visualization of a successful image can create a mental imprint of success and increase the likelihood of repeating that success.

TIME FOR MASTERY

Effective visualization can be immediate or take several weeks of practice to master.

VISUALIZATION EXERCISES

The following visualization exercises will help your child develop imagination skills to reduce physiological stressors and enhance the likelihood of repeating successful performances.

How to Visualize Effectively

It's imperative that you not practice these skills while using electronics, operating a vehicle, or engaging in potentially harmful activities. The optimal method to develop these skills is in a controlled and quiet setting, where you and your child will not be disturbed. When you become more advanced with these skills, you will likely be able to practice in more diverse settings.

(1) Loosen any restrictive clothing, and lie down on your back with your arms and legs stretched out flat.

(2) Close your eyes softly and begin deep breathing.

(3) Scan your body, seeking tension in specific muscles. Relax those muscles as much as you can.

(4) Form mental impressions involving all of your senses: sight, sound, smell, touch, and taste.

(5) Use affirmations by repeating short, positive statements that affirm your ability to relax in the moment. Use the present tense and avoid negatives such as, "I don't feel anxiety" or "I'm not tense." Instead use positives such as, "I am loose," "I am relaxed," or "My body is calm," "I am at peace," or "I can quiet my mind."

Visualize at least three times a day. Visualization practice is easiest in the morning and night while lying in bed. After some practice, your child will be able to visualize while waiting for class to start, before a test or presentation, or minutes before competition.

There are three types of visualization that you can practice with your child: Programmed Visualization, Guided Visualization, and Successful Visualization.

PROGRAMMED VISUALIZATION

This entails creating a scene with pre-determined details you tell your child to visualize. For example, you can take your child through an exercise of how you specifically want him to clean his bedroom by giving him the details of how the room should appear when it is clean. You provide the details of how the bed is to be made, how the clothes on the floor get hung up or put in the hamper, how the shoes go in the closet, and how the toys are put away. This can be used for any activity—from school to chores to sports, and everything in between—for attaining a goal.

GUIDED VISUALIZATION

This exercise provides the framework of a scene and allows your child to fill in her own imaginative details. For example, you can ask your child to visualize her safe place. Ask her to imagine what makes her place safe. What does it look like, sound like, smell like, feel like, and taste like? Guided Visualization will help develop your child's imagination and can be used to enhance positive memories or bring to life desired outcomes.

SUCCESSFUL VISUALIZATION

When repeatedly practiced with deliberate focus on how successful performance will be achieved, Successful Visualization will create an imprint in your mind. When the opportunity arises to engage in that imagined performance, you will more likely recall the mental imprint of success and repeat what you have imagined. Below is a Successful Visualization script I've used to help young athletes develop a mental imprint of successful performance.

Have him/her lie on his/her back on something soft, with bent knees and feet about shoulder width apart. Make sure the spine is straight and arms and hands are resting at his/her sides. Then read the following script:

Close your eyes and take a deep breath in. Hold that breath for a count of 1 ... 2 ... and slowly exhale. Again, repeat the deep breath in, hold it for 1 ... 2... and slowly exhale. Continue with your deep breathing to gradually slow your heart rate and increase your focus on calm, easy breathing. With every breath you feel more calm and more relaxed. With this feeling of composure and relaxation, allow your body to release all tension, worry, and muscle pressure. Free your mind and body from every restriction.

Allow yourself to feel relaxed and your body to freely exist. Continue your normal breathing. As I count down from 5 to 1, you will find yourself becoming more and more relaxed. You're in control of the process and you control how relaxed you want to get. There are many safe places for you inside your mind. 5...you're relaxed and you're comfortable ... 4 ... you're feeling calm and composed ... 3 ... allow yourself to freely float within your feeling of peace ... 2 ... you're at peace ... 1. (Pause for about 5 seconds.)

With your feeling of comfort, peace, and self-control, remember a moment in your life when you accomplished one of your goals. Remember the pleasures of your accomplishment. Maybe it was a successful competition, an excellent performance, or a rewarding interaction. Envision yourself at that time ... Allow yourself to go back to that moment and relive that positive experience ... Recall your moment of success in vivid detail. (Pause for about 5 seconds.)

Recall what the environment looked like ... What was going on around you at that time ... Recall the time of day ... The clothes you had on ... Remember what you were doing at that time and what made the experience a success ... What did you do to be successful? ... What images do you attach to your success? ... Do you recall any aromas that correlate with your success? ... Is there a taste that goes along with your success? ... Recall the sound of your success ... This was a powerful moment in your life that generated positive feelings of accomplishment, reward, and success. Secure these feelings and any others that you relate to your success. When you recall these positive feelings, you'll be able to generate these desirable emotions and relive your feelings of success. Through your emotions you can generate the positive feelings and energy to succeed. These are your emotions, your actions, and your ability to be successful. Take a moment to enjoy your success. (Pause for about 5 seconds).

Now envision the success that you want to occur in your present life. Imagine yourself going through the preparation for success. Go through your prepared routine ... Allow yourself to feel the adrenaline rush and anticipation for your performance ... As you feel prepared and ready to perform, take a deep breath in and hold it for a count of 1 ... 2 ... and slowly exhale ... Allow yourself to experience the current moment, being aware of what your body comes in contact with ... What you are able to touch ... All that you can see ... The sounds within the environment ... What you can smell ... What taste you have in your mouth ... And the powerful emotions of feeling prepared, competent, and confident in your abilities to succeed.

You have relaxed your mind and body, and successfully used imagery to prepare yourself for a rewarding performance. You are competent, confident, prepared, and ready for success ... It's now time to perform!

Appendix

Centered in Performance

These are skills that I've found help reduce stress and pain, and when implemented into training and competition, help achieve successful performances.

Progressive Muscle Relaxation (PMR) – tense and release

(1) Clinch teeth and release

(2) Shrug shoulders to ears and release

(3) Tighten fists and release

Try to stay away from major muscle areas that will be used in performance to avoid the possibility of cramping.

Breathing to Release Tension and Quick Calm

A. Breathing to Release Tension

(1) Sit or lie in a comfortable position with your arms and legs uncrossed and your back straight.

(2) Take a deep breath into your abdomen. Hold it. Exhale.

(3) As you exhale, count "one" to yourself. As you continue to inhale and exhale, count each exhalation by saying "two ... three ... four."

(4) Count your exhalations in sets of five for 5–10 minutes.

(5) Notice your breathing gradually slow down, and feel your body relaxing and your mind calming as you continue to practice this breathing exercise.

B.　Quick Calm

(1) Sit or lie in a comfortable position with your arms and legs uncrossed and your back straight.

(2) Take a deep breath into your abdomen, saying "I'm calm."

(3) Hold it. Exhale saying, "I'm relaxed."

(4) Continue this pattern of deep breathing for 30–60 seconds.

(5) Notice your breathing gradually slow down, and feel your body relaxing and your mind calming as you continue to practice this breathing exercise.

Centering

(1) Firmly secure your feet to support your weight.

(2) Take in a deep breath.

(3) Focus on one objective (explosive block start, consistent rhythm, quick feet, explosive hips).

(4) Release the breath.

(5) Commit to the action.

For example: A swimmer standing on the block or holding onto the wall before the start of a race will take in a deep breath, focus on how he will explode off the block or wall, release the breath, and anticipate the start.

Effectively Use Attention and Distraction

(1) When to pay attention in the moment:

- When the coach is talking and giving instruction
- Warming & cooling down (jogging, biking, stretching, etc.)
- During moments of performance (executing a play, doing a drill)

(2) When to use distraction to relax:

- Prior to performance to avoid wasting energy (imagine completing a successful performance)
- Between drills when you're not receiving instruction (practice effective breathing)
- During scheduled breaks in performance (allow your mind to wander or imagine your next successful performance)
- When performance is over (imagine enjoying your recovery or recalling what you learned in performance)

REFERENCES

Ebihara, O., Ikeda, M. & Myiashita, M. (1983). Birth order and children's socialization into sport. *International Review of Sport Sociology*, 18, 69–90.

Flowers, R. (2000). Effects of sport context and birth order on state anxiety. Kansas City, MO: University of Missouri–Kansas City Press.

Schachter, S. (1959). *The psychology of affiliation*. Stanford, CA: Stanford University Press.

Acknowledgments

I must begin by giving a huge THANK YOU to my editor Stacey Aaronson for skillfully bringing my thoughts together. She is a pleasure to work with, and I highly recommend her to anyone interested in writing. She lives up to her moniker as The Book Doctor (www.thebookdoctorisin.com).

The idea for this book started with one of my closest friends, who for years encouraged me to always write about my experiences, and, if possible, share them to teach or inspire others. Thank you Bruce Strothers for planting the seeds and nurturing the soil for my writing. Many close friends shared suggestions and feedback through the development of this book. Thank you Jamahl Powell, Luther Carr, III, Kali Roberts, Shawn McWashington, Dr. Wendy Borlabi, Dr. Tracy Shaw, Dr. Margaret Ottley, Quentin Givens, Morell Jones, Jr., Joe Mills, Percy McCreight, and Chris Johnson.

A special thank you to my youth coaches who taught me sound fundamentals through sport. Thank you Raphael Rachman, JoJo Rodriguez, Al Hairston, the late Frank Ahern, and Fred Beckwith for your commitment to teaching and for challenging me to be better. As a student-athlete at UCLA, my fundamental skills were tested through years of critical decision making and growth. Thank you to my UCLA coaches Bob Larsen, John Smith, Dr. Tommie Lee White, and Art Venegas. Dr. White is the first person I knew who used the title Sport Psychologist; he also happened to be my hurdle coach at UCLA. What an honor to have a great hurdler not only teach me to be a better hurdler, but also how to improve my mental and emotional skills. That was a bonus. Thank you Dr. White for the introduction to sport psychology and for your encouragement to use my temperament, ability to relate well with others, and understanding of sport to pursue a doctoral degree and become a psychologist specializing in sport and performance.

From his years of success at UCLA as the head track and field coach, to being a 2008 Olympic Track and Field Coach, to coaching Meb Keflezighi to win the 2014 Boston Marathon, Coach Bob Larsen has been a consistent model of performance excellence. He demanded the best from me as a student-athlete and UCLA men's track and field team captain, and I am honored that he offered his endorsement and words of recommendation for this book. Thanks, Coach!

It was surreal to see Meb Keflezighi win the 2014 Boston Marathon, one year after he was at the finish line seconds before the terrorists' bomb exploded. To know Meb, our connection as UCLA Bruins, his journey to success, and his pursuit of fulfillment made his victory even more meaningful to me. Meb, thank you for continuing to run and for giving me your support for this book.

At UCLA, I had the pleasure of watching and training with many of the world's best track and field athletes, which greatly enriched my college experience. I still marvel at the fact that I shared the track with one of the greatest female athletes of all time. Jackie Joyner-Kersee delivered an undeniable example of how to execute power, speed, and grace with sound fundamentals. Thank you, Jackie, for continuing to inspire me through your dedication to youth development, for your encouragement and motivation, and for your generous endorsement of this book.

When I suffered a severe leg injury in college and the threat of not being able to compete anymore, I was fortunate enough to meet Dr. William Parham. Bill's ability to relate, his understanding of sport, and his agreeable delivery of useful knowledge was—and still is—very timely. Thank you, Bill, for being a leader, mentor, and friend who set a memorable example of how a sport psychologist can create a bridge between counseling psychology and athletics on a college campus. Thank you for challenging me to be more than a student-athlete and for sharing your wisdom and support as I left my comfort zone to embark on a doctoral degree. I deeply appreciate your ongoing mentorship and the guidance you gave as I developed an applied sport psychology program at UC Davis.

Leaving southern California to pursue a doctoral degree in Kansas City, Missouri, was no easy task. My advisor, Dr. Chris Brown, provided expert guidance and helped me keep my sanity and sense of humor while completing my degree. Chris was instrumental in helping me to find my path and to keep moving forward. When I arrived at the University of California, Davis, Dr. Emil Rodolfa was the director of Counseling and Psychology Services (CAPS), Greg Warzecka was the Athletic Director, and Pam Gill-Fisher was a Senior Associate Athletic Director. I was fortunate to receive their direction and encouragement to create an applied sport psychology program. Thank you Greg, Pam, and Emil for giving me a blank canvas and allowing me to paint freely.

Some of my greatest experiences occurred while I worked with the United States Olympic Committee. While attending numerous competitions and traveling countless hours to extraordinary locations, I met fantastic people. It really is unfortunate that we only get to know our Olympians every four years because these are great people in sport, performing their best every day of every year. I feel fortunate to have met some amazing athletes and coaches around the world through sport. Two amazing people I would like to acknowledge and thank are Apolo Anton Ohno and Chad Hedrick. Thank you for your support and for not forcing me onto the ice!—and thank you both for your generosity in writing an endorsement for the book.

One of my closest colleagues in sport is Al Joyner, Thank you, Al, for continuing to compete and for sharing your golden nuggets of coaching on and off the track. You are the epitome of a positive person with a generous heart. You inspire me to be better, and I am truly grateful for your friendship.

In the process of writing this book, I received incredible motivation and stories from the parents, coaches, administrators, and athletes with whom I've had the privilege to work—many of whom are a part of the city of Chula Vista Recreation Department and athletics programs, King Sports Worldwide, Olympians and Olympic hopefuls, San Diego State University, and administrators, coaches, and athletes in Trinidad & Tobago. A special thank you to all of the SportOutlier Foundation parents, athletes, and sponsors who have participated in training camps and clinics to inspire and develop youth through sport.

Most importantly, this book would not have been possible without reinforcement from my family. My mother, Micki Flowers, and her twin sister, Vicki Giles Fabré, delivered instrumental feedback that helped me express my thoughts and enabled me to convey my unique journey in this book. My father, Robert Flowers, not only coached me as a youth athlete, but is my most dominant and consistent positive role model. He is cut from a unique cloth that I aspire to wear one day. Most younger siblings strive to match or at least challenge their older siblings. My older brother, Dr. Christopher Flowers, has always set and achieved a high standard of success. He did that when he skillfully guided me to one of my early athletic titles—a story featured in the book. He is also setting a wonderful example of how to father three healthy, happy, balanced student athletes. Now, as an associate professor of hematology and medical oncology at the Emory School of Medicine, he continues to inspire me. Thanks, Chris.

To my sources of unconditional love and endless inspiration, Anthony, Ayden, and Christian—thank you, sons, for your patience and positive pushes. We pray together, play together, and stay together. I love you boys!

About the Author

ROSS FLOWERS, PHD, is an experienced psychologist with expertise in elite performance who consults around the world with culturally diverse athletes, coaches, teams, athletic departments, athletic national governing bodies, military, executives, and business organizations. He also teaches, designs, and implements skills development programs for national and international performance.

Ross has served at the Associate Director level of the United States Olympic Committee as a senior sport psychologist, as well as on many USA World Cup, World Championship, and Olympic teams with USA Track & Field, USA Canoe/Kayak, US Speed Skating, and US Biathlon. His prominence in the area of elite performance enhancement is supported by his background as an elite athlete, NCAA Division 1 coach, and executive coach to local, national, and international business organizations seeking individual and organizational performance enhancement.

As founder and director of the Applied Sport Psychology Program at the University of California, Davis, Ross worked in Counseling and Psychological Services and the Intercollegiate Athletics Department. Ross holds a doctorate of philosophy in counseling psychology from the University of Missouri–Kansas City with emphasis in performance and sport psychology, and a bachelor of arts in psychology from the University of California, Los Angeles.

Additional information about Dr. Ross Flowers and services he provides are available through his website:
www.GilesLLC.com
or on Twitter @GilesConsulting

Integrating Successful Performance Services

CPSIA information can be obtained
at www.ICGtesting.com
Printed in the USA
LVHW081314250419
615536LV00014B/298/P

9 780996 108218